The Saviour of the World

Volume V: The Great Controversy

Charlotte M. Mason

Routledge
Taylor & Francis Group
Routledge Revivals

First published in 1911
by Kegan Paul, Trench, Trübner & Co. Ltd

This edition first published in 2015 by Routledge
2 Park Square, Milton Park, Abingdon, Oxon, OX14 4RN
and by Routledge
711 Third Avenue, New York, NY 10017

Routledge is an imprint of the Taylor & Francis Group, an informa business

Publisher's Note

The publisher has gone to great lengths to ensure the quality of this reprint but points out that some imperfections in the original copies may be apparent.

Disclaimer

The publisher has made every effort to trace copyright holders and welcomes correspondence from those they have been unable to contact.

ISBN 13: 978-1-138-90097-4 (hbk)
ISBN 13: 978-1-315-70034-2 (ebk)
ISBN 13: 978-1-138-90098-1 (pbk)

Routledge Revivals

The Saviour of the World

The Saviour of the World covers each incident and each saying in the Bible and converts them to either a single poem, blank verse or rhymed stanza, according to the subject. This volume, called *The Great Controversy*, was originally published in 1911. This book will be of interest to students of both religious studies and English literature.

Photo, Braun *Titian*

THE SAVIOUR

THE SAVIOUR OF THE WORLD

VOL. V

THE GREAT CONTROVERSY

BY

Charlotte M. Mason

LONDON

KEGAN PAUL, TRENCH, TRÜBNER & CO. LTD

BROADWAY ... LANE, E.C.

Printed by BALLANTYNE, HANSON & Co.
At the Ballantyne Press, Edinburgh

PREFACE

Having reached the middle of a great (and bold) undertaking, may I be allowed again to offer my *apologia*?

It is not because I "relish versing," or with any hope to give pleasure to persons who care for poetry, that I am essaying to throw the life and teaching of our Lord into the form of verse; but because, under that progressive teaching which we believe is vouchsafed to the Church, a new need appears to have arisen, in response to which many efforts worthier than mine are being made.

Day by day we are taught to pray, by way of summing up all our requirements in this life, for "knowledge of Thy truth"—the prayer in the Liturgy which seems to summarise most fully our Lord's teaching. But our practice hardly keeps pace with our prayer; we are apt to put two or three legitimate desires before what should be our primary aspiration; to *have* good—the cult of prosperity—is the prayer and effort of the natural man; to *be* good—the cult of sanctity—is the desire of the spiritually-minded; to we do so after critical examination, applying the only appropriate standard, that is, the Personality of our Blessed Lord; the intellectual labour we have given makes the conception our own, and we have gained some fragment of that knowledge which is eternal life.

If we reject the proposed rendering, we are in still better case, because we do not do so without such labour of thought as gives us another conception of the situation, another interpretation of the saying, and so our religious life becomes vivified by a further realization of the Divine Person; thus, the verse rendering will have served its purpose as a point of departure.

I think we must bear three things in mind in study of this nature: that we build upon the foundation which is laid—the teaching of the Church[1]—for no Scripture is of private interpretation; that we have no special thesis to advance, but are open to "receive with meekness the engrafted word"; and that our reading be not casual,—as though one were to dip here and there into a book of mathematics,—but continuous, following the chronological order of our Lord's life rather than the sequence of events as given in any one Gospel: only so shall we be in a position to realize the progressive and cumulative character of the Christian philosophy proposed to us.

[1] The Church, *i.e.* "The blessed company of all faithful people."

The present volume, for example, deals largely with controversial passages, which some of us are apt to put aside as irrelevant and perhaps a little tiresome! But this controversial matter makes up a large part of the "all things" "whatsoever" Christ has spoken, and a line-upon-line study here appears to disclose aspects of the divine character and teaching peculiarly suited to modern life. Christ stands before us labouring painfully and incessantly to make men *know,* understand; He tells the Jews, that truth makes a universal appeal; that every one has power to discern the truth when it is put before him; that men must before all things be candid, think sincerely. We can hardly read these chapters in St. John's Gospel devoutly and continue to allow ourselves in the random-thinking, leading to vitiated conclusions, which spoils so much of life.

Little or no attempt at textual criticism is made in these volumes, because we are probably approaching an era of yet "Higher Criticism," based upon a truer apprehension of the Divine Person; and towards this Higher Criticism every devout study is a contribution.

The part played by "the disciple" hardly requires explanation: the disciple is any devout reader of the Gospel history who must needs, inadvertently, play the part of the Greek Chorus by offering such "authentic comment" as the occasion calls for.

The Church possesses an illimitable field of literature—sermons, commentaries, expositions, hymns,—including all the ground I am attempting to cover; but perhaps every new presentation is a gain; and it may be that the gradual progressive development of Christ's teaching can be advantageously set forth by way of paraphrase and amplification in the rarely attempted form of verse.

CONTENTS

BOOK I

OF FORGIVENESS

BOOK II

THE GREAT CONTROVERSY

BOOK III

THE WATER OF LIFE

BOOK IV

THE LIGHT OF THE WORLD

(The Great Controversy)

BOOK V

CHRIST, OUR LIFE

LIST OF ILLUSTRATIONS

CONTENTS OF VOLUME I

THE HOLY INFANCY

ANGELS and prophets long had searched in vain
Those mysteries, now, for wayfarers writ plain:

How Christ was born in Bethlehem of pure Maid,
How to three kings His Rising was displayed:

How holy Simeon blessed Him and foretold
His Mother's grief, He, sacrificed and sold.

How out of Egypt did God call His Son
That all the prophets figured might be done.

How, simple Child, He dwelt in Galilee
That simple folk His light might daily see.

How to Jerusalem in His twelfth year
He went, before Jehovah to appear:

How there He shed His light, a duteous Boy,
To keep the law His errand, not destroy.

How eighteen years of meek submission then
Prepared Him for His labours amongst men.

How He went out to John to be baptised,
And John in Him a greater recognised.

How in the wilderness for Forty Days
He bare assaults of Satan. Give we praise!

How in Caná He made the water wine,
That men should see of life in Him a sign.

How in Jerusalem quick drave He forth
The traders and their wares—of how small worth!

How journeying north to Galilee once more,
He sate and taught that Woman heavenly lore.

How all the men came out who heard His fame,
And, SAVIOUR OF THE WORLD, *did Him proclaim.*

These things have we considered as we might,
And hence would meekly follow in His light.

CONTENTS OF VOLUME II

HIS DOMINION

"At even ere the sun was set," they came
To Him for healing, sick and blind and lame.

Then wearied, He, a great while before day,
Went out to desert place that He might pray.

The folk of Galilee would make Him King;
He knows how little worth the praise they bring.

Weary with preaching, Christ bade put to sea;—
Behold, a wondrous draught, the fishers' fee!

A leper cried, Thou canst,—wilt make me clean?
I will, saith Christ; healed, who had leprous been!

Levi took customs' dues by the seaside,
And when the Master called, he straight replied.

His Jews rejected for hypocrisy;
Too skilled in subterfuge, what hope have we?

Man at Bethesda's pool so long had lain—
The Lord who healed him to betray was fain!

Christ taught,—the Father and the Son were One
In words They spake, in all works They had done.

On the Son the royal crown of judgment set;—
He learned the ways of men, nor would forget:

In Him was Life; and all the souls that live
Draw breath from Him, to Him their praises give.

The Law, the prophets, witness; to each heart,
The Father testifies, and shows his part.

Thy Jews condemned, grant us, good Lord, to heed—
Unstable in our faith, slack in our deed!

Christ walked in cornfield on the Sabbath day,
And set men free from bondage whilst they pray.

He instantly the withered hand restores,
And, grieved, the Rulers' faithlessness deplores.

Once more to fair Gennesareth He came,
And multitudes drew nigh, with love aflame.

Our Founder chose the Twelve, and laid them, sure
Stones to sustain that Church which shall endure.

He charged them; told them, how the poor are blest;
How persecutions should their lives molest:

Taught them the brother-secret; how to give;
How with all men as brothers they should live.

Of blind man led by blind man, cupboard's store,
Of building House of Faith, He told them more:

And then He climbed the Mount that all might hear,—
That multitude had come from far and near :

" Blessèd are they that mourn," He told the sad ;—
With promise of the Father's care made glad.

Chaste must they be and kind and guard their speech ;—
For God's own holiness is in man's reach.

He taught men how to give their alms, to pray ;
And all their anxious fears to put away.

Behold, the Church He founded on that day
Received those Institutes should guide her Way.

The people heard, and hardly understood,
But knew the Word He spake was very good ;

Perceived Authority in every word
And fain would bear due fruit of that they'd heard.

CONTENTS OF VOLUME III

THE KINGDOM OF HEAVEN

Who knows the things of God and doth not tell,
Like him who hides a lamp, doth not do well.

Together are let grow the wheat and tares,
Till each kind to its place the reaper bears.

Thou think'st to watch the growing of the seed?
A secret, that,—so by God's will decreed.

A grain of mustard-seed, so small to see,
May yet become a mighty sheltering tree.

Thou'st found a treasure? Go and sell thine all,
Ere thou this treasure all thine own may'st call.

The woman hid the leaven in her flour;
The Word hid in a heart shall rise with power.

A merchant came upon a pearl of price
And forthwith bought—by liberal device.

And, "Have ye understood?" the Saviour cried;
"Yea, Lord," they said, but in their lives denied.

"Thy mother and Thy brethren would Thee see;"
"These be My kinsfolk—they who follow Me."

Proud Nazareth rejected Him who came
To save the humble: Do not we the same?

Jesus came walking o'er the stormy sea;
His friends, relieved, were there—where they would be.

The demoniac raged as fierce as angry storm;
Christ spake,—and meek he sat who'd wrought such harm.

The little maid was raised by Jesus' hand:
"Now, see ye no man tell," the Lord's command.

A woman crept behind and healing took;
Christ made her happy by a pitying look.

Two blind men came and cried on Him for sight:
The Lord restored to these the joys of light.

A dumb deaf man sat moody by the way;—
Christ taught dumb lips to praise His name that day.

The time had come to send the Twelve abroad,—
Bless'd messengers to carry forth the Word.

As father charges son would cross the seas,
So Christ, their Father, gave His charge to these.

"Dangers I see await you on your way;—
Be prudent, friends, and bide a better day.

But have no fear; knows not your Father all
Of good or ill His children shall befal?

Yet ye must bear the cross, nor shrink in shame
From any obloquy or any blame.

Of this be sure, whoever you befriends,
Your Father in heaven will make that man amends."

Forth fared the Twelve in pairs to do His will,
And as they went, the Lord was with them still.

With joy these men returned to shew their Lord
How it had prospered with the seed, His Word.

Now, John the Baptist prisoned in strong tower
To chide the king had used a prophet's power:

The king sware foolish oath to grant what boon
The princess asked of him; vindictive, soon—

"Give me John Baptist's head," she cried; and, lo,
The sorry king bade armèd men to go

And bring the prophet's head. The news was brought
To John's disciples; quick they Jesus sought

And told their grief to Him. "Come ye apart,"
Saith Christ to the weary Twelve; with tender heart

They follow Him and tell what things befel
In all the cities—whether ill or well.

CONTENTS OF VOLUME IV

THE BREAD OF LIFE

"Come ye apart into a desert place:"
But, quick the folk the Master's steps to trace:

All day the Master spake; the people heard,
And hungered while they listened to the Word.

"Give them to eat," He said: and one produced
A meal scarce more than one *to eat was used.*

Christ blessed and gave to all that multitude
And all were filled with meat—and gratitude.

He bade His friends take ship; then sent away
The folk, and climbed the mountain there to pray.

A storm arose; He looked and saw them row
Their little craft while wild the winds did blow.

He walks upon the sea ; they take Him in ;
Instant, subsides the tempest's fearful din.

Next day the people seek Him in the place
Where He had fed them amply by His grace.

Returned, they question Him ; and mysteries,—
The work of God, the bread of God,—to these

Unlearnéd He discloses ; shows them how
God gave the manna as He feeds men now.

Having made plain that life-sustaining bread
Must ever come from God, He turned and said,—

" I am the bread of life ; who eats of Me,
That man alone eternal life shall see."

His disciples were offended : " How can He
Give us His flesh to eat ? Can such thing be ? "

Many forsook Him and fled ; the Lord was grieved :
" Will ye, too, go away ? " they who believed

Were asked in sadness : one stood up and said,—
" Thou hast the words by which a man is led

In the ways of life; to whom then should we go?"
Peter, that happy saint who answered so.

"Nay, you Twelve have I chosen, and one of you
Is a devil:" said the Lord, whose word is true.

He told of things which most defile a man;
Not casual soil, but evil which he can

Conceal in his heart while outwardly he's clean;
But his foul secret thoughts by God are seen.

Nor shall one unto God that portion give
Which he owes to his father—that the man may live.

He journeyed northwards to the coasts of Tyre;
A woman came with passionate desire

That He would heal her daughter, sorely vexed;
Nor at His chiding did she go perplexed,

But spake that word of faith the Lord approved,
And He healed the little daughter whom she loved.—

"The dogs," she said, "the crumbs that fall may eat,"
And Christ received her at His mercy-seat.

A dumb-deaf man they brought; He touched his tongue;
"He hath done all things well!"—the people sung.

Again, a desert place the Saviour sought;
The people followed and their sick folk brought.

Three days they listened to the Master's Word;
Ah, blesséd folk who on the mountain heard!

Once more He fed them from a trifling store;
They ate till none was willing to eat more.

Before and after that great word of BREAD
Which HE IS, *the Lord the hungry people fed;*

That none might say, "Such Bread's a thing of nought;"—
Unlike the daily bread men ate and bought.

CHRIST *and the Twelve land at the sunset hour;*
Men ask a sign to manifest His power.

The sign of Jonas,—is the Lord's reply;
From those unfriendly shores with haste they fly.

"Beware of the leaven of the Pharisees,"
He bids the Twelve; and they their Lord would please,

And chide themselves that they had not brought bread
Enough in the boat for each man to be fed.

The blind man of Bethsàida they brought
To Christ, who took his hand and led him out

Apart from the rest ; cured him in stages three,—
In each of which a parable we see.

They journey north,—a pilgrimage oppressed
With coming woe—towards Hermon's snowy crest:

And, on the way, foretelling grief and loss,
He bids the Twelve go forth and bear the cross.

"He that will save his life, that life shall lose;
He saves his life who doth not death refuse."

And now He takes the three and climbs the mount
With heavy steps the weary men scarce count.

The Lord knelt down and prayed: the Twelve went, sleep,
Too weary loving watch with Him to keep.

They waked, and, lo, the Lord was seated there,
Shining and glorious—most exceeding fair!

And two spake with Him, men of royal mien;—
Persons so noble no man yet had seen:—

Moses and Elias, come to cheer the Lord,
Before His coming conflict, with the Word

Writ in the Scriptures for Him to fulfil,—
Accomplishing in all the Father's will.

A sudden cloud enwrapped the glorious sight,
And the three, scarce sensible for joy and fright.

As they descend the mountain, lo, a crowd,—
A wretched father cries on Him aloud

To save his son, possessed; Christ drave them out,
The demons who had brought this ill about.

They left that region, sore oppressed with grief;
For Christ had brought home to their slow belief

The great things He must suffer, and the pains
They too should bear,—full gladly for all those gains

They found in Jesus and the words He taught:
Now, tardy steps the heavy pilgrims brought

To the house of Peter, there, in Galilee,—
Capernaum, fair city by the sea.

One came to Peter for his temple dues;
"Half shekel, too, your Lord will not refuse."

"Go to Gennesareth and cast a hook;
Draw the first fish to land, nor pause to look:"

He went, and in its mouth a shekel found,
And paid those dues on every man were bound.

When all were in the house, now hear Him say,—
"What matter, then, discuss'd ye by the way?"

They were ashamed, for, Who should be the first,
Was their dispute; and none of them now durst

Confess his fault: Christ took a little child,
And looking round with loving aspect mild;—

"Look on this child; humble yourselves as he;—
Behold, the greatest in the kingdom, ye!"

Of peace, of salt, of many things He spake;
Of certain woe should that man overtake

Who scorned the little children, hindered those
Whom the Lord cherishes because He knows.

And as a limner draws stroke here and there,
And every stroke reveals the aspect fair

Of him the painter limns, so these perceived
The grace of Him in whom they had believed

Produced in clearer outline by each word
Which sorrowful, yet glad, they meekly heard.

"My heart is inditing a good matter: I speak of the things which I have made to the King."

BOOK I

OF FORGIVENESS

THE
SAVIOUR OF THE WORLD

I

Of forgiving our brother

Of offences, salt, the mystery of a child,
Of humility and peace, had spoken the Lord:
The words He spake searched hearts as strong
    March winds
Search out weak places in a feeble frame:
One and another came with a case too hard
For him to determine: this one asked the
    Lord:—
"My brother, Lord, hath spoke ill words of me,
And one, a friendly neighbour, came and told;
What for his trespass shall I do to him?"
"My next-door neighbour hath encroached on
    me;
He blocks my doorway with unseemly things,
His children hinder who would enter in?"—
So said another, full of sudden wrath:

A third spake hot,—"What, to a man who cheats,
Who takes day labour from men nor will pay?"
And all the crowd were eager, each man's face,
Hot and distorted with excess of spleen,
Shewed murderous hate within; and each disclosed
The wrong or outrage most was festering there,
In the hidden place of his heart; they looked on Christ,
Knew them in presence of the JUDGE, serene;
Amid contending tongues, all unperturbed;
Their clamour ceased; the calm of JUSTICE spread
In troubled hearts; each knew his cause was safe,
And waited, meek, the verdict of the Lord.

One word He spake to all, for each had come
With tale of offence 'gainst him by brother wrought:
"What shall I do to him?" was all their cry:
And, lo! the offending brother, not the man
Who bore the offence, was in the thought of Christ,
For his, the greater need. A new thing, this,—
The injurer, not the injured, is the wronged;—
"Poor man, he has injured thee? Nay, what of that?
Consider thou the wrong he does himself

In wrong he makes thee suffer: see'st thou not
How warped his judgment, selfish, hard, his
heart?
Nay, know'st thou he can find no place to pray?
A veil is between him and God; a stubborn
wall
'Twixt him and all the tenderness of men,—
The while that wrong he's done thee 's in the
way:
Haste thee to help thy brother in ill case!

"But, say'st, 'Nay, he has done the wrong, not
I!'—
His sin's his need; his offence cries out for help,
As were he drowning or his house on fire;—
How would'st thou succour him in such distress!
I say to you, this poor man's case is worse:
Who wrongs his brother builds an adamant
tower
About him, which excludes all warmth of love
From sun in heaven—as from neighbour's fire:
Poor wretch, he perisheth, a prisoner:
Haste, then, with quick release and let him
out."

Dismayed, they heard: then, soft forgiveness
stole
As light o'er the dark world; sudden, each saw
The pitiful case of him who had done the wrong;
And knew in his heart,—'twere better to endure

All injury than commit the offence of him
Who hates the brother that hath done him
wrong.
"But, Lord, he is proud," saith one, "how make
him know
That I bear no grudge, would have him free
himself
From bitterness of bondage?" "Go to him;
Shew him his fault 'twixt thee and him alone,
Nor neighbours call to witness to thy wrong,
Nor prate of his offence about the town:
Simple, sincere, and loving him, he sees
Thee come, and knows thy candid soul desires
His restoration only; he repents,
And thou hast gained thy brother: well is
thee!"

"But, Lord, if he be sullen, will not hear—
For scarce have I been gentle—what do I?"
"Take with thee one or two to strengthen thee;
To restrain thee, too; men are not rash of
speech
When, serious, they before witnesses confer:
But, see thou gain thy brother; all thy part,—
Kind, courteous, to convince him of the truth:
Flinch'st thou? Perchance thou wert not always
right?
Hap, violent words have 'scaped thee, scornful
looks?
If thou hast wronged thy brother, tell him so

Before thy witnesses; then, moved, will he
Own his transgression, and thy brother's gained."

"If, Lord, he have in truth done me a wrong,
Nor have I aught to blame myself withal,
If he refuse to hear, though meek I come,
Nor receive my witnesses, good Lord, what
then?"
"There be offences of malicious dye,
Wrought unprovoked, and suffered silently,
For th' offender's hardened to all just reproof,
Nor can resentment reach him. In such case,
After thou'st tried and failed, go, tell the
Church:
The Spirit of wisdom rests on two or three,
As on multitudes, collected in My name:
The Church shall counsel take, hear evidence,
And let the offender speak: righteous decree
Shall issue from My Church, in meekness set
Not her own will to do. Should, then, the man
Stiffen his neck, regardless, thou no more
Canst do to save the offender; let him be
As open sinner, pagan,—nought to thee:

"But beware thou hasten not this sinner's doom
Through thine own arrogance; 'tis thine to save,
Or damn, to bind or loose the man; he goes
Henceforth as thou'st propell'd him—saved by
love
Or by thy harshness hardened; bound by heaven,

Or loosed, as thou hast willed." They heard in fear;
Who might dare cherish wrath if a man's soul,
Here and in heaven, hung upon his love,
And he, so quick to hate! The Lord perceived
How truth wrought in their souls, who stood condemned
Of loving not their brother.—
"There is a way
Whereby thy brother's soul may yet be saved
And thou escape condemnation. If two of you
Agree on earth as touching anything
They will to ask, behold, My Father's ear
Is open to their prayer; it shall be done—
That thing the two shall ask; for I am there,
In their midst, where two or three are met to pray;—
The boon they ask is theirs."
With lightened cheer
The disciples heard this word, as men relieved
From the guilt of brother's blood: for who would let
His brother perish when his prayers might save!
And each resolved to pray, and thought in his mind
Of the two or three should help him in his prayer:
As dungeon sudden opened to broad day,
Was their heart,—in instant vision, wonderful,

OF FORGIVENESS

Of the omnipotence of prayer, as magic sword,
Able to cut all knots men's hate had tied.

And Peter, apt to test this weapon new,
Invincible, this brand in heaven forged,
His Lord had girt upon him, cried in haste,—
Ready to show a fond excess of love
For sinning brother,—"How oft shall I forgive,
To-day, to-morrow, until seven times,
Shall he against me sin, and I forgive?"
"Nay," said the Lord, "thy measure's scant, My
friend;
Till seven times seventy shall thy brother sin
And thou make haste to pardon. No limit draw
To the forgiveness brother to brother owes."

Though all the powers of heaven at their hest,
Dismayed were the poor men: they knew them-
selves,—
How quick to wrath, to mercy, ah, how slow!—
And, fearful of the tasks the days should bring,
Tasks of forgiveness exceeding their poor might,—
"Increase our faith," they cry, "Lord, give us
help!"
And the Lord, tender to His own, told tale,
Which, as shutter opened to the east, should
throw
The light of heaven on men's little wrongs.

II

The two debtors

A LAVISH Eastern King one day
Thought his poor kingdom was the prey
Of greedy courtiers, unjust lords,
Who seized upon those fair rewards
Merit alone should claim, and spent
As they were kings themselves, nor lent
Of all their wealth for public use,
Or rid the land of one abuse.

"I'll call a reckoning," cried the King,
"See what account these lords will bring,
Of wealth they gather as for me,
But spend in rout and revelry."
He set his scribes to work, and scarce
Had they begun their task, than worse
Than all imaginings, appeared
The debts and frauds the King had feared.
For one poor wretch no good they bode,
So numerous, vast, the sums he owed:
Day after day they laboured on
This great lord's schedule; when 'twas
done—

Photo, Mansell & Co. *Rembrandt*

THE UNMERCIFUL SERVANT

Each item reckoned in a sum—
The very lawyers were struck dumb!
Ten thousand talents! sure his head
As well as wealth were forfeited!
In millions sterling, we should name
The debt th' accomptants must proclaim.

The satrap stands before the King,
An abject wretch with nought to bring,
Not even poor excuse, for all
That wealth he'd lost beyond recall:
To his scribes the King said, "Sure, ye err!
What say'st to this accompt, good sir?"
The trembling wretch had ne'er a word
To propitiate his angry lord:
"What hast to say for all this waste,
What recompense to offer? haste!"
"I've nothing, Lord, to bring to thee,
Of all wherewith thou'st trusted me!"

Then turned the King to his chief lord;—
"Hear'st thou his self-condemning word?
Nought has he of that vast estate
I lent him; he has runagate,
And pleased himself at lavish cost
With wealth to my poor kingdom lost:
Go, gather all to him remains—
The palaces, gardens, he retains,
His servants, children, e'en his wife;
Nay, sell himself,—I spare his life."

And, lo, a sound of weeping 's heard ;—
Men listen for the broken word :—
" Have patience, Lord, and bear with me,
And all this debt I'll pay to thee ! "—
The wretch cried, sobbing, at the feet
Of the great King he dared entreat
For pardon, promising to pay
When nought he had, or hoped, to lay
Before his offended Lord.
But he,
Distressed the man's distress to see,
Bade let him go : released, forgiven,
Sure that man dwelt—one hour—in heaven!

No sooner was this satrap freed,
Than seeking how to meet his need,
He thought who owed him any sum,
And bade all these before him come :
One poor wretch owed a hundred pence,
And, quick, for that so small offence,
He seized him by the throat and cried,
" Pay that thou owest ! " He denied
Intent his fellow wrong to do,
And vowed he'd pay in season due :
His fellow-servant had no ruth
But cast him into prison, sooth,
For little debt he soon might pay
Had he been left at liberty.

But not unmoved his fellows saw
This wrong done to their friend. The law

Might give this cruel lord the right
To treat his fellow with despite;
But he was a servant, too! they ran
With their complaint of this hard man
To lay it before the King: he heard,
And wrath and sorrow moved his word:
"Have I not just forgiven thee
That debt immense thou owed'st me?
I thought that thou would'st mercy shew
To him who aught to thee should owe:
Thou hadst no pity for distress,
Nor would'st with love thy brother bless:—
Go thou and pay the penalty
Of all the wrong thou'st done to me:
Forgiveness for him is there none,
Who forgives not wrong to him is done."

The disciples heard with awful dread
The accusing word the Lord had said:
For the first time, each saw unrolled
Those debts, tremendous, manifold,
He owed his KING, most merciful,
Who gave forgiveness, bountiful
As the early rains, to wash away
Record of all he could not pay!
Forgive his brother? Nay, he'd run
To pardon him had trespass done
Against him: how else could he shew
A heart with gratitude aglow

For that abundant pardon free,
Had saved him in his misery?

"Forgive ye not your brother's sin,
Then have ye never hope to win
Forgiveness at My Father's hand
Of all that debt He will demand.
The utmost penalties remain
For them, their brother's debts retain."

III

Christ walked in Galilee

Ah, blesséd country, how thy paths are dear
To us who love the Lord! Is never spot
In all that northern province but His feet,
Weary with walking for behoof of men,
May there have trod: we wonder that 'twas so—
That the Son of Man a footsore pilgrim went,
And all for love of us! As bride thou go'st,
Thou many-floweréd Galilee, arrayed
In memory of Him who walked in thee!

Jerusalem drew the Lord, for there was set
His Father's House resplendent upon Zion!
How fain would He go up with them that praised!
But enemies lay in wait in Zion's ways,
And, went He up, the end had come too soon.
His own received Him not; as Outlaw, went
The Christ of God, the King of Israel,
E'en as that King who, hunted, hid himself,
A partridge on the mountains!

See, festive pilgrims gladden all the ways,
Songs of high praise and merry jests go round

Among the folk, embower'd in branches green
They carry to Jerusalem there to build,
Each family, its booth of verdant boughs:
A moving forest, went the merry folk,
And gleeful children played and women sang;
But Christ who loved the people might not join
Their happy ranks for them that sought His life.

IV

His brethren

James. Good Brother, to Jerusalem go'st with us?

The Lord. I go not up.

Judas. Now there, Thou'rt wrong; we've watched
These many months to see what came of 't all,—
Thy teachings, healings, journeyings to and fro:
Time was, men heard amazed, and thought, "In truth,—
Here is Messias, walking in our midst!"
(The foolish ones are swayed by any breath!)
But now, disciples drop away from Thee;—
What wonder? Waiting is dull work at best.

James. To the Feast with us and all the congregation!
There, do Thy works,—some cure that shall convince
Physicians and the people: inform the Scribes,
The Pharisees, those who have wit to judge,
Of the doctrines Thou dost teach!

The Lord. Believe ye not?

Simon. Nay, who are we to judge? Wherefore, I say,
Come to Jerusalem now and test the case:
Who knows, the fickle people may return,
And hail Thee, king of the Jews!

Joses. Or, if not that,
Thine old disciples, seeing Thee once more,
Once more drawn to obedience by Thy voice,
May gather round, a goodly company!
Nay, think of us in this; is't good to hear,
"Thy brother, what of Him? He goes alone,
Or with scant following, who erst drew crowds:"
Nor add they, "As we said 'twould be,"—for, see,
A hand stretched scornful speaks th' unuttered word;
That a man dishonour thus his father's house,
Give men's tongues leave to wag,—this is not good.

James. Joses saith well; come, justify Thyself
In Jerusalem where be those apt to judge:
What comes of works performed in secret here
In quiet Galilee's hid villages?
A man is known by his works: he who would be
A great one 'mongst his people, why, he works
Before the eyes of the multitude; men see,
And hail him, a deliverer.

So spake they,
Resentful, that in nought were they the more
In men's esteem for all the works of Christ.
Ah, how our "virtues" hurt us! We think well

Of him would advance himself, his family;
"A worthy man," say we, "and will get on:"
Nor see we that a ring of brass shuts in
That man's horizon who wants no more of life
Than that he and his should prosper. "If thou dost
These things," say they, "go, shew Thyself to men!"—
And these, the brethren of the Lord, who had seen
Those works of love and pity wrought by Him
On many a friend and neighbour! "*If*," they say—
From chiding to contempt is an easy way,
And things they'd seen with their eyes, they knew no more,
Nor were assured of, till on them was placed
The seal of authority; till Pharisees,
Learned scribes, proud priests acknowledged Him. Do we
Dally with doubt, not certain that we know,
For anguish of doubt has pierced us to the soul;—
Or,—We, we would not hold what others doubt
And they, the authorities who needs must know?
So Scepticism skips light and unashamed
Into souls that own no serious fealty.

No more in honour held, His soul abased
By every grating word that shewed these men

As aliens to His purpose—remote from Him,—
The Lord is *acquaint with grief:* not even
they,
His brethren, who beheld His blameless days,
Heard words of power, saw acts of tenderness,
Not they, His own, believed or understood!
To hurt, not move, the Lord, their words had
power;
For other laws ruled all His Times—His hours,
Due numbered and appointed; not for Him
To move on His way until the time had come—
Time other than they dreamed, those men
compact
Of certainties learned of the world. His Time?
How had the ages laboured to bring forth
The Time so close approaching! How, hence
forth,
Should ages lift eyes to the culmination
Of all desires, the solace of all griefs!
And these—they thought to haste the time of
Christ
With their puerile hopes and fears!

THE LORD. My time is not come,
Not yet; who waits on God, in seasons fixed
His service shall perform, nor shall he know
Till summoned what the hour requires of him:
For you who serve the world there is no pause:
Your time is alway ready, and ye must watch
Lest rich occasion slip by unemployed,

And the world's wages pass you, negligent.
So, go ye up, my friends; a welcome, find,
For the world hateth not her followers;—
She hateth Him who convinceth her of sin:
Not yet shall I go up, but bide Mine hour,—
My time is not yet fulfilled.

V

The Lord goeth up

So spake the Lord, nor knew His brethren then
The significance of His word : "time to go up,"—
Thought they, obtuse, when Christ spake of
 "My time ;"
Nor knew of consummation to be wrought
On Calvary upon a certain Day—
Day, not forestalled by any wilfulness.

So having said these words, He lingered still
In Galilee while all the folk went up :
Then when the roads were quiet, Christ came
 forth,
And sought Jerusalem by devious ways—
(On the other side of Jordan ?)—An Outlaw, went
The Lord of all,—as man on whom price is set :
Ah me, the Man of Sorrows ! had He where
To lay His head those solitary nights ?
Did any give Him bread, or hungered He,—
Those days He trod the wilds,
Towards Jerusalem, "in secret as it were" ?

VI

The Feast of Tabernacles

As bride adorned for her spouse, Jerusalem
Sits queenly upon Zion. Blossoms red,
Fruits golden, verdant boughs, she decks her with,
Deft wrought by practised fingers—booths of joy,
Planted on roofs or whatso vantage coign
Quick eyes discern to hold an edifice,
Built as the birds build, for glad family.
At noon and eve the silver trumpets ring—
Blown by two servitors from the marble steps—
And Israel's faithful heart takes up the cry,
"Towards JEHOVAH, LORD, our face is turned!"
City of Palaces exceeding fair,
Jerusalem shines for her ten thousand guests
Up gathered from all lands to serve the Lord.

Fairest where all is fair, the Temple stands
Resplendent on Moriah: they behold
An edifice of gold and snowy white,
Of magnitude unequalled, vast, immense,
Wonder of beauty, glowing in the light
On that high place towards which they turn
eyes—

The moving throng—each bearing citron bough
With fragrant fruit, and palm branch held aloft
To screen eyes from the hot October sun;—
The lusty sun which had ripened all that wealth
Of mellow fruit and golden grain brought up,
An offering to Him who had filled that cup—
Held in the hollow of His hand—their land!
The people sing and dance before the Lord:
But what of them,—the priests and Pharisees,
Masters of these high ceremonies? Proud,
They gazed on all the jubilant scene, assured—
"This, this, the People's life! This shall endure,
These altar-rites and these high Festivals,
So long as God is in heaven, and Israel thrives—
Scattered among the nations, yet increased!"
So solace they their hearts for many a fear,
Dark doubt, sudden dismay, had fallen on them
During those anxious months now overpass'd.
See, arrogant, they tread the marble courts
Engaged in their high functions; lofty, sweep,
With sanctimonious pride through crowded streets
Where huddling men make room nor dare to touch
The hem of their broidered robes. How well was all!
But was it well, indeed? To what intent
Those furtive glances shot from watchful eyes?
The ministering priests in trepidation scan,
Even they, the movements of the multitude:
Say, what uneasiness disturbs their pride,
What look they for, these high ones?

VII

The people talk

MEETINGS and greetings, hurryings to and fro,
Comings and goings, exchange of family news,—
Was ever scene so animated, gay?
But not all given to mirth and jollity,—
The crowds that throng the City: see them sing
And play before the Lord, what time they catch
Some ruler's supercilious glance; saith he,—
"No mischief brews behind the staring eyes,
Wide mouths of the fool-people! All is well!"
No sooner turns he than folk talk again
In whispers, glancing fearful round the while;
The shifting crowd resolve them into groups,
And all groups canvass, keen, the selfsame
theme:—
"What think ye, will He come?" "Nay, for
the Jews,
Our Rulers, lie in wait;—see ye yon man,
Watching, as cat a mouse? and yon? and yon?
They're servitors of the temple; everywhere,
Scattered among the folk, they lay an ear:
'Who be His followers?' ask the crafty priests,—
And, mark you, things shall go but ill for him,

Who follows Jesus, named, of Nazareth!
What hope for Him, then, should He dare come
here?
But He knows better—take my word for that!"
"But He's a good man," said a grateful soul
Whom Christ had raised from lingering sick
bed,—
"Not worse than you or I, or other folk."
"Good friend, thou art misled," a sleek man
cried,
Who knew it behoved him to keep well with
those—
The Rulers of Israel who dealt out fat things,—
"Be not deceived by manifold good works
And ways of holiness; he doth but mock
The people, easily led; have ye ne'er heard,—
False prophets shall arise and lead astray
Them who give ear?"
That none in all that crowd,
Where thousand souls had known the ease of
words
Dropped cool and healing on the burning spot
Of sin-wrought misery, where thousand frames,
Diseased, had known His touch, where many
men
Had followed Him, disciples for a while,—
That none should up and say, "He is the Lord,
That Son of David, should deliver us!"
"No worse than the rest of us, a worthy man,"—
Behold, the limit of their poltroon praise!

And we—we who 've heard words that quicken'd
us,
Have passed through days when, "Lord, Lord!"
was the cry,
Saved us from madness, we who *know* indeed,
Holding this secret knowledge of the Lord—
The light, the fire, the comfort of our days,—
Yet do we dare presume, judicial, cold,
To weigh the claims of Christ,—"Certes, He's
good,
The best of human kind, let's say; no peer
Has risen to Him of Nazareth since time was:
But to suppose Him more than man, why, that
Would rank us with the credulous, ignorant:
This our last word,—'He's a good man, be sure!'"

But what say these? "Leadeth the multitude
Astray, giveth laws the Rulers know not of,
Should make the people free—each man sus-
tained
By other meat than we wot of, set at large
From the thraldom of those laws that fetter
men,—
Nay, let them know they be of small account,
The common people!"

VIII

Christ comes

And while the rulers lie in wait,
And people watch with idle prate
Of, Will He come or will He stay?
Or, Sure He'll fall a certain prey
To the machinations of the Jews—
Not they the men such chance to lose:—

While the people wait, half hope, half fear,—
Lo, Christ is there! Illumining, clear,
As the light of day His presence seems:
That gracious presence on them beams,
Revealing, cheering, chiding those
Who, unconscious, stains expose

Before the silent Light: men haste
To gather round Him; who would waste
A chance of hearing words, the Jews
Would have men to their hurt refuse?
So in the portico they walk,
Christ and the multitude: His talk,

They strain full eagerly to hear:
But why are all His words so dear
To the callous crowd of late so cold,
Now, sudden grown impassioned, bold,
Nor caring aught what they may do—
The haughty priests and all their crew!

An Outlaw, Christ had come at last
When three days of the Feast were past,
And the jealous Jews had ceased to ward
The city gates with sedulous guard:
But not in byways stood the Lord,—
In the Temple's self, men heard His word:

Aye, all men heard; His captious foes,
Afraid to touch Him there with those,
His followers about, lent ear;—
Hap, some stray word may yet appear,
Dropped casual, shall serve to accuse
This Man of guilt before the Jews.

BOOK II

THE GREAT CONTROVERSY

Luini

CHRIST AND THE PHARISEES

By permission of The Autotype Fine Art Co. Ltd., 74 New Oxford Street, London, W.C.

IX

In Solomon's porch

THOSE men of letters, well equipped to deal
With heresy in subtlest guise, believe
An easy task is theirs;—this Galilean,
Unlettered peasant, how shall He withstand
The arguments of the Schools, chisell'd to point
Through age-long use of Doctors of the Law?
They hear, amazed: "Whence hath this peasant brought
The learning of the Schools He ne'er has known?
How knoweth this man letters? Literate,
Able to set forth ordered argument,
Yet having never learned—a wonder this!"
Ah me, the Light is there in noontide blaze,
But their gross darkness comprehendeth not:—
As blind men grope they, those enlightened priests!

The Lord (smiled He at their high-learned conceit?)
Spake:—"I, too, am a Schoolman; I have learned:
Not an illiterate come I to instruct:

Mine is the greatest school by Rabbi taught:
He that hath sent, instructed Me: hear Him:—

"Ye scan My doctrine, heresy to discern?
With all your searching ye shall not perceive—
Not had ye all My words before your eyes—
What is it that I teach: nor can I shew
An I would, My doctrine to your blinded eyes:
Not by much learning, not by subtle arts,
Shall men these lessons learn; the wayfarer,
Though a fool, shall not err therein; but ye,
For all your scholarship, shall not perceive:
Behold, I stand to offer every man
The knowledge that shall save him; free displayed
Before his eyes that doctrine: comes he to take?
'Tis in a casket held, inviolable,
Locked sure 'gainst all save him who hath the key:
Not the learning of the schools this key may forge;
The man who comes with desire, as a starving wretch
Craves loaf from baker's basket, he doth *will*,
And he shall know of the teaching: witness sure
Shall come to him, that words so fit for his case,
Poor fainting soul, are the very words of God:
That man shall know I speak not of Myself:
But ye, who nothing lack, ye have no will,
No want, My words shall appease—how may ye know?"

X

The Voice consummate

(*The disciple*)

Insistent voices clamour for our ear:
This—hath a trick of sweetness, soon might cloy;
That—wily reasonings knoweth to deploy;
And all have tones—offensive, heard too near.

One Voice there is—constraining, mild, austere:
Those Jews in the Temple heard a Man deliver
Word of such round completeness, they might
never,
For all their learning, make one flaw appear:

We wonder not at their perplexity,—
"This skill in dialectic—whence hath He?"
Should men, thought immature, from Jesus hear?

"A dreamer, this," they might not mock and say;
Nor "One who dully practiseth the way!"
How excellent Thy Words,—O Lord, how dear!

XI

He that willeth shall know

(The disciple)

STILL that great Controversy's at our door:—
"What proof have ye that we may see and know,
What truth demonstrable have ye to shew,
That we convinced go hence, nor vex us more?"

"No demonstration, or for sight or mind,
Hath Christ left with us; truth, shall we discern
By the light of the steadfast will, light pledged to burn
More radiant, the more intricate we find

The passage of the Word." "Ye juggle, then,
Believe what ye choose, nor are impell'd to learn
Truth at all hazards,—ignorant, fond men!"

"Nay,—ye thresh air with flail, with trowel, turn
To lay on sunshine: fit tool to use, we ken;—
To labour with good *will* is our concern!"

XII

The test of truth

Priest. "Willeth—shall know"—we know not what He saith!

THE LORD. In that thou hast spoken true—thou knowest not!

This quest of proof confounds thee—ocular sign,—
Nor know'st that deepest things of love and life
May not be proven: man hath higher tests—
He knows to seize the truth when it appears;
One flash of conviction shows the whole of life,
And the man goes forth as Abram, leaving all:
This knowledge is for him who *wills* to know;
Not I, but He that sent me, teacheth this.

Priest. We thought as much; He magnifies Himself,—

As though the Word of God came to such as He!

THE LORD. Who speaks of himself, he seeketh his own praise;

What have I sought of you,—your wealth, esteem,
That ye should hold Me learned, a mighty one?
I only among men am He that serves;

None other is meek in all his inmost thought :
But I have an office to sustain ; I come,
The Ambassador of God ; to honour Him,
To glorify Him among men, come I :
In My Sovereign's Name, I claim allegiance.

More wrath were they with Him for th' searching word
Which rebuked their arrogance ; each knew in his heart
Of strife for triumph, pride of intellect,
Urging that nought is true, nor shall be true,
But what is proved by methods recognised
And followed by the learned : more was amiss ;
How *will* the Will of God when personal ends—
Accredited position, wealth, good name—
Be willed with all the will a man can urge ?
The will is one—as a man's soul is one ;
Who wills his own advancement, what hath he
Wherewith to will God's Will or know the truth

XIII

Right judgment

Priests. Ye have the law of Moses: hear Him not!
What room in your lives for any other law?
By the Law of our Fathers shall we live and die,
And—death to him who scorns it!

THE LORD. Ye do well
To deal out death to one who breaks the law;—
"Thou shalt not kill," is written; wherefore, then,
Go ye about to kill Me? Is this the law?

Confusion seized the Rulers; was it known
To Him, their plot to kill Him? Who had told?
Never a word they answer. But the crowd,
The multitude of pilgrims come to the Feast,
Ignorant of the private counsels of the Jews,
Of secret movements guiding State affairs,
Respecting, too, their rulers,—raise the cry;—

The Crowd. Who goes about to kill Thee? delusion,
Far-fetched and monstrous, hath got hold of Thee!
Tak'st Thou our Rulers for assassins, then?

Thou hast a devil who makes believe a lie;
Nay, fight against possession, see the truth!

Mild with the multitude, He made reply:—

THE LORD. Nay, understand, My friends, what thing ye cry!
These say, I break the law; for the law's sake,
My death they compass. How break I the law?
Ye saw Me to make whole an impotent man:
"It was the Sabbath," say you; what of that?
To make a man whole every whit, is't worse
Than to wound, that one may circumcise, his flesh,
When both be on the Sabbath? Unlearned, ye—
(Tender the Master's tones and pitiful,
As of one who would upgather in his arm
A little helpless child exposed to wrong)—
And they, the rulers, mock you as untaught,
A swinish multitude: they'd think for you,
And bid, Go here, or, there, Do this, or, that,—
And never heed your cry of "Wherefore, then?"

My friends, not this the part your Father set
For each of you: not thus may ye hand o'er
Your proper function; to each man I say,—
A task is set for thee, none else can do;
A task, not of set labour with thy hands,
But of true thinking with the mind thou hast:

Ye shall not judge by the appearances of things,
Nor let persuade, by specious arguments,
Your learnéd men, who know to make good, ill.

Take heed to what I tell you;—each of you
Hath lodged within him power to discern the right;
Judge righteous judgment; considered in that light,
Which an honest man finds thrown on problem dark
When he seeks to know the truth, all becomes clear:
Examine yourselves, and see if I be true,
Ere, intemperate, ye cry, "He hath a devil!"

XIV

In perplexity

(*The disciple*)

My Lord, I would ease me
Of a burden that oppresses me;
Why should I not ease me,
When, urging about me,
Are the valiant and mighty, all eager to bear
That burden to me is—a harassing care?

The air's thick with questions,
And all mightily concern me:
Old laws, shall they rule me;
New guides, shall they steer me?
Now, how ascertain I if the elders were right,
Or if I for safe walking must go by new light?

One hastes to assure me,—
"Hardness has passed away for thee;
Glad precepts shall rule thee;
Gay guides shall direct thee;
High Sanction has passed from the words of the Book;
But go thou not fearful—as though God-forsook!

"We, we will sustain thee;
With New Thought we will uphold thee;
Course light, buoyant, give thee,
As of bladder in air.
We know what is in thee; we've noted thee well;
Thy way would we ease as by magical spell.

"Fear not, 'tis no new thing
We tell; Christ hath acquainted thee,
That all things are for thee,
But as they appeal to thee;
We come to thee, wretched, release to proclaim:
We're bold to deliver in Christ's holy Name.

"Nothing is ill with thee
Till thine own mind so shews it thee;
Think nought's amiss with thee,
Believe all is well with thee,—
Lo, sickness, anxiety, vanish at touch
Of a faith that knows how, in the Lord, to claim much!"

. . . . . .

Thus, Lord, they come about me;
These new prophets, to flout me,
An will I not yield me,
An try I to shield me
From clamour of teaching strikes false on mine ear;
And their way is so easy! But, I fear, Lord, I fear!

"Thou shalt not thus ease thee;
Nor let their foolishness please thee;
Use th' insight given thee:
What would they do for thee?
Make easy and effortless the days as they go,
Or bid thee live strenuous that thy God thou may'st know?

"Well, child, dost thou guard thee
From facile tongues which would deceive thee:
But My truth shall keep thee—
My truth that is in thee:
Full well thou know'st, though a coward and weak,
That the glory of God is the end thou shalt seek."

XV

The townsfolk take up the controversy

They of Jerusalem had marked the crowd,
Those country pilgrims, toss the ball about—
The question concerning Jesus, nor gave heed;
Sure, better-informed, they, and knew the
 facts
Which the multitude spent idle guesses on.
But the Lord's word arrested them: all men
Have that within which answers when one
 cries,—
"Fair play is all I ask!" "Judge righteously,"—
Said Christ; and straight, they asked themselves
 in doubt,
"Is His offence so certain? What know we?"
Now, see, immediately, a tribunal's called;
The men in the street—the judges—hear the
 case,
And one and another urges plea that counts.
First Citizen. These strangers don't know all
 that's going on;
They think this Rabbi's mad for guessing well
That the Rulers seek His life; we know about
 that.

Second. They've compassed heaven and earth to seize the Man;
I have it on authority; my kin,
Some two or three, are Temple servitors,
And they've been bribed to lie in wait for Him—
A heavy price to the man who brings Him up
Before the Sanhedrin! What do they then?
Take my word for't, my masters, He'll not live!
He opes His mouth and all the folk lend ear,
And every word of His, as battering-ram,
Shatters some bastion in that edifice
Of practices they've built up in God's name.
'Tis as if God Himself had come to purge
His House of error.

Third. Here's a curious thing—
We know they've sought Him up and down the land,
And there He stands, and none lays hand on Him!
Explain me this. Would'st say, the finger of God?

Fourth. Aye, that's the point; our rulers, do they know
That here is indeed THE CHRIST? We've waited long,
These thousand years and more, to see His face—
And, what if the COMING ONE indeed hath come
And speaks with us in His Temple?

Fifth. The wonder of 't! But dare the Jews
conspire
Against Jehovah's Self, and knowingly
Put the Messias to an open shame?
See you, He speaks what all men know is true;
And they, convicted, say nought in defence,
Nor venture to attack Him! What means this?

Sixth. Nay, my good friends! Ye go too far
in your zeal;
The Man speaks marvellous words; I will admit
That all we hear of Him proclaims His praise;—
But, see, He claims too much; allow His words,
And, where's the Temple ritual, nay, our life?
Our rulers must safeguard the things of God,
Nor let him live who attacks.

Seventh. Aye, we know
That the rulers of the people be good men,
Patterns of righteous living, free of alms,
And holy men of prayer; why, any day
You see them at street corners, lifting voice
To God on high, as in His confidence;
Would such as these, think you, plot to deprive
Their people of the Prince who should be our
Peace?
Why, it were infamous that our teachers, *they*,
Should make the promises of none effect,
Whilst the Nation lives on hope! That were
too base!

Sixth. Our ignorance is in fault; but knew
we well

The Scriptures of our people as do they,
We'd have assurance that this is not the Christ,
E'en as our rulers have ; look you at this,—
"The Lord shall suddenly come to His temple,"—
now,
No glorious sudden coming's here ! His ways,
All His poor living down at Nazareth,—
These things be known ; not our Messias, this !

XVI

The Lord makes answer

THE Lord, discerning all the thoughts of men,
Noted the vehemence of this group remote,
And cried to them afar,—teaching and saying ;—
" Aye and indeed ye know Me,—know My kin,"—
(Not pausing He to show wherein they erred,
Nor how in Him the rays of prophecy
Were focussed as upgathered light in lens :
The letter killeth ; Christ sought other ways,—
Assumed as true that which they held as true,
Raised them to higher levels, other thoughts :—)
" Say, then, ye know Me and know whence I
came
As one man knows another ; there is more
To know than ye perceive. Out of Nazareth
Come I ? Yea, but forth from your God I come
To discover Him to you—who is the Truth.
I come not of Myself ; I am sent forth
To shew, in ways that men may apprehend,
The Truth of God. Then, wherefore do ye err ?
Why think false thoughts of Me ? For this one
cause,—
Ye know not Him that sent Me ; knew ye God,

Not thus erred ye in judgment. How know I?
Ye mocking ask :—With knowledge surer yet,
More intimate, than spouse hath of his spouse,
Than child of mother, I, Jehovah, know,
The Father from whom came I ;—He hath sent ;
And knew ye Him, Me ye would comprehend.

XVII

Willing and knowing

(*The disciple*)

"*If any man willeth to do His will he shall know of the teaching, whether it be of God.*" (*R.V.*)

WORKING the Work, willing the Will!—Thou art
A Teacher of mysteries! 'tis of Thy might
We're able, O our Lord, to get by heart
These lessons of Thy setting, in despite

Of all that heavy dulness 'tis Thy task
To lighten with Thy glorious countenance;
Till th' inert *will* drop from us as a mask,
And, quickened, wake we, as man out of trance.

For what the secret, then, of willing well?
To keep the single eye, to think on *Thee*,—
Till seeing Christ, our lightened heart shall
swell
To that vast measure, His Humility!—

Then of Thy doctrine we in truth shall know
When all our will is—in Thy way to go!

XVIII

The country-folk, the citizens and the Jews

THE city folk, the country multitude,
All heard Christ witness,—"I am sent from Him
Who is your God; ye have the gift to know
The truth when ye hear it, an ye will: believe
The word I speak, nor think in yourselves a
lie:"

And, of them all, the country-folk believed:
Candid, they asked themselves: "When Christ
shall come,
Will He do greater signs than those we know
This Man hath done among us?" And one told
Of little child brought back from the door of
death:
A second, "See these limbs, e'en strong as yours,
And I, would ye believe 't,—had palsied lain
For many a year before He came and—healed!"
Then one, whose absent eye dwelt on the past
With tender gaze and fond,—"I was of those,
He fed that first time He brake bread, and gave
To multitudes—meat scarce enough for one."
Most men had heard or seen or known somewhat

Of how, like the Sun in his might, the Lord had
gone
With healing on His wings about their coasts—
And many believed on Him.
The city men
Were slower of response; their bread, see you,
Was concernèd in this matter; turned the Jews
From this one, that one, with offended brow,—
Why, what of wife and children, wages gone?
And, for men try to hold as truth that lie
They live by, these upheld the probity
Of the men they served with loyalty misplaced.

And they, "the Jews," what of them? Every
man
Is tested by the response he makes to truth:
Not dead in them the power to hear and know,—
Man's chief inheritance; and those dread words,—
"I know Him, I am from Him,"—found them out.
Then came they straight—and bowed before the
Lord,
As the Kings who came to His Rising?—Alack,
for them!
A thousand sophistries had place with them,—
Their learning served them ill: "A mischievous
Man
Who stirreth up the people"—they avowed:
With restless haste they called their servants
up—
Those willing janitors,—"Go, fetch ye Him,

And it shall be well with you." Ready, they
went:
They came to Christ, but laid no hand on Him,
And spake no word; His time was not yet come;
Invisible Power, deterrent, held them back,
(As thou and I be held from urgent harms):
The chagrined rulers watch the multitude,
And hear the praise of Christ on every lip:
More officers send they forth, and still in vain

XIX

The warning

THE Lord looked on, aware of thoughts that worked
In many, then;
And most His pity for who most had need—
Those stubborn men,
Indurate to the truth, which as water flowed,
And subtly urged
Its way into all hearts not doubly barred
There, where truth surged.

Pitying, Christ looked on them, the foolish men
Who fought against truth:
"Now is your opportunity; no more,
Look for God's ruth:
Now, for a little while, I am with you;
Bethink ye, proud,
That while I am with you, ye may yet repent;
Yea, cry aloud

To Him Who pleads with you—not for His life,—
Ye may not touch

A hair of His head to injure—till His time—
Little or much.
Not for My sake, but yours, I lift Mine hands
As one distress'd,
And pray you to take pity on your souls,—
Choose to be bless'd!

For, see you, I go hence to Him that sent;
And on that day,
Your doom is sealed; no place is left for you
To turn and pray!
Distresses shall fall on you, awful dooms;
Your desolate cry,
Then, "Where is He besought us to believe,
Lest we should die?"

On that day of your anguish, ye shall cry,—
"Nay, where is He,
Invited us to turn and seek His face?
Now, fain, come we!"
It is too late, My friends; ye have your times,
Even as I;
Where I go come ye not; nor elsewhere find
A Saviour nigh.

XX

Where goest Thou?

(*The disciple*)

Our Lord, where goest Thou? we too would
know:
As babe who sees his mother borne away,
And stretches hands and cries on her to
stay,—
So are Thy people, hearing,—Thou wilt go!

Where art Thou all this while we cry on Thee?
Distresses manifold beset our way;
We see Thee not, yet cry on Thee and
say,—
"For we are friendless, Thou, our Succour be!"

To be alone, how awful! There is none
Comes nigh us in that solitude, is left
When Thou departest, leaving us bereft:
But knew we where in space our Lord is gone!

Then would we rise and follow Him with haste,
  Would catch the hem of the robe He used
    to wear,
  Would make Him pity us for that despair,
Came on us out there in the lonely waste.

. . . . . .

"My children, ye do err, nor understand
  That, not removed am I to any place
  Remote from him, in meekness, seeks My
    face;
Lo, I am there, in every time and land:

As loving mother holds out tender arms
  To shield her little one when danger's near,
  So do I cherish these my children dear;
Yea, shield them from all perils and alarms.

But, see you, place doth not condition Me;
  I am and I am not in any place,
  To them who seek not, them who seek, My
    face:
The wilful, proud, and stubborn shall not see!"

XXI

The Ambassador withdraws

How solemn is the scene: the mighty crowd
Is silent, as perceiving issues great
Hang on that controversy 'twixt Christ and them
Who ruled in Israel. Their hatred grown,
These bade their men,—"Go, take Him at all
costs,
E'en should a riot call the legions out
And cause the heel of Rome to trample us."

And, "therefore," Jesus spake: but why, "there-
fore,"—
We, timid, ask:—conceive we *posse*, then,
Of city officers sent to apprehend
Some royal prince in our streets, who comes to
pay
Visit of honour in his father's name—
And, lo, as one disorderly, they seize
Our princely visitor—those officers
Whose business 'tis to deal with rude offence!
Conceive! but how conceive we the awful scene
When the Person most august, the Son of God,
Come on behalf of God to visit men,

Thrice royal Visitant, was thus misprized!
Christ, answering, arraigns these haughty Jews
For rude infringement of His Majesty:
His credentials He withdraws: "I go away
To Him that sent Me." Could Ambassador
With more dignity, finality, retire?

XXII

"What is this word that He saith?"

MIGHTY is truth and shall with men prevail!
The man confined by the letter—of what avail
Is truth to such an one? He hears, believes,
For he needs must: but every man receives
According to his measure; can but know—
As his own limitations prove it so:

That Christ would go, evade them, they were
sure;
These ways of His,—how patiently endure?
The more they think on't, more they vex their
heart,
And cry to each other, "How shall He depart,
And whither goes He that we shall not find?
In every city men fulfil our mind,
Perform our messages, further our views,—
And this man vainly thinks He can refuse
To submit Him to us! Whither will He go?
To the Dispersion among the Greeks? Soon
shall He know,
So far, our arm can reach Him: to all Jews,

On the shores of the Great Sea, we'll send out
news
Of His coming, and their part; will He teach
the Greeks,
Or Gentiles abhorred of the Law? (how the
name reeks!)
Well may this outcast wend to such as these,—
Their heathen orgies, hap, His soul shall please,—
He who contemns the Law, nor honours God!"
And all the while they writhe as under the rod
Of His correction; cannot get away
From word—of going hence—they heard Him
say;
In passionate irritation mouth it o'er,—
"What is the word that He said?" Cry they,
once more,
With scornful finger-play and glance of hate;
"'Me shall ye seek nor find Me,'—Is't too late?
'Where I am, come ye never'?—pray, why not?
Who, then, shall hinder us, and who hath got
The right to bid,—hence go, or, hither plod,—
To men who hold the oracles of God?"

For all their proud derision, in their heart,
They knew the Christ full surely would depart.

XXIII

Keep back thy servant from presumptuous sin

(The disciple)

Is'T true that I,
In controversy with the Son of Man,
Lift up my voice, outreach my puny span,
And hold me high,

As one who had right
To question with Very God, and make demand,—
I, insignificant, held in His hand,—
To mock His might!

To lightly hold
The very words He spake as of small account,
Nor weigh them well nor reckon their amount?
I am too bold!

How dare I go,
Exalting my poor wisdom over His,
Preferring mine own way, refusing His!—
My salt tears flow

For mine offence!
"My Spirit shall not always strive with man,"—
And Thou hast wrought with me since I began!
O, go not hence!

BOOK III

THE WATER OF LIFE

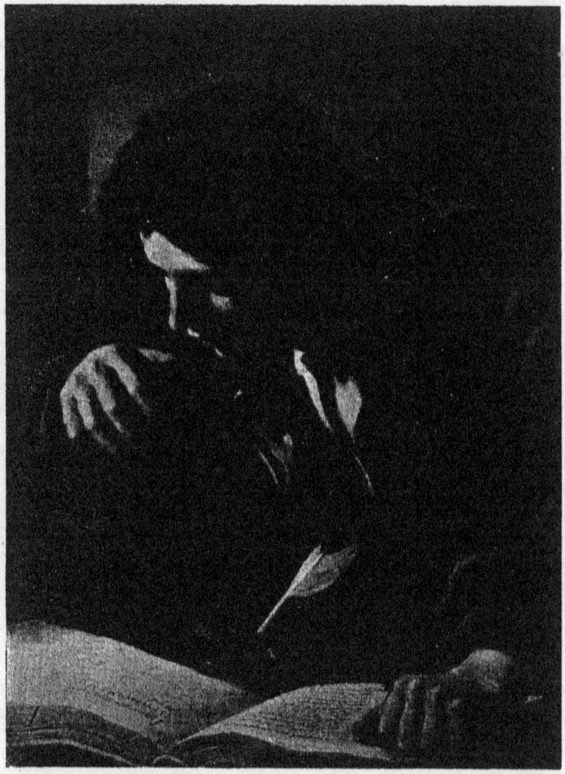

Photo, F. & D. Brückmann *Il Guercino*

S. JOHN WRITING HIS GOSPEL

XXIV

"Ho, every one that thirsteth!"

Now, what know we of thirst, who dwell
Within reach alway of a well?—
We draw and quench our modest thirst,
Nor pause we to consider, first,
How bounteous, blessed, our supply;
Nor think of them who fainting lie,
Their sinews withered, blood dried up,
For lack of the life-giving cup.

There was a man had ridden long
In eastern desert: there, among
Ravening wild beasts, he couched at night;
But not of these was his affright;
Four days they'd journeyed since the last
Bless'd hour of water-drinking 'd passed
Swelled tongue, dried sinews, blackened skin,
Witnessed to burning drought within.
This western man fared worse than they—
Of the desert—used athirst to stay.
Behold, an object, distant still,—
A mirage—trees and wells at will?
Nay, as they journey it remains
Nor fades away o'er the wide plains;

But the man faints ere yet they come
To this so grateful desert home;
One opens mouth, another pours
Delicious stream; his parchéd pores
Begin to moisten, eyes to ope,
His frame to expand with life and hope:
In after years, he told his friends,—
"I drank, drank, drank; no drink that ends
Would seem to satisfy my need;
Continual flowed, with tranquil speed,
The water into me; my veins,
The thickened blood again sustains:
My shrivelled skinny hands expand,
My skin, no more like leather tanned,
Perspires, grows moist; refreshment fills
My parchéd body—bless'd by rills
Of living water coursing there;
My soul was rescued from despair!

"That day I knew, as ne'er before,
That *water* only could restore
To life a famish'd fainting wretch:
No matter whence the drink we fetch,—
White, from cow's udder, take our draught,
Or blood of purple grape gay quaff,—
'Tis water still our life preserves;
Water all our occasions serves;
And water, pure, sans taste or hue,
Can best a fainting wretch renew."

XXV

The vision of the holy waters

The prophet,—dry of soul and much distressed
For the arid hearts, lives fruitless, dry, unblest,
Of his people, Israel,—was cheered of God:

Pure waters saw Ezekiel issue forth
From underneath the Sanctuary, flowing north,
East, south,—whichever way the prophet looked.

One took his hand and brought him through
the stream;
Up to his ankles, did the waters seem
To rise abundant; nay, up to the knees;

Now, to the loins; and, still, the waters rose;
A stream to swim in through the desert flows:
And he who swam drank life at every pore.

Carried in safety to the river's brink,
He notes how all the creatures come to drink;
How goodly trees on either bank spread boughs.

All ills are healed where'er the river flows;
See, life-dispersing, cheering, on it goes;
And multitudes of fishes swim therein.

And trees grow there with never-fading leaf,
And plenteous fruits for hungry men's relief;
The leaf shall heal, the fruit, all souls sustain.

XXVI

Christ stood and cried

THAT last great day, when Israel took down
booths,
When many sacrifices brought to the priests
By them were offered; when the joy of the
Lord
Filled as new wine the hearts of all the folk—
Jesus stood and cried:—
The eastern teacher sits,—but Jesus stood;
Spontaneous came His words, impassioned, not
To be repressed His urgency of appeal:
Nor sate He, but with arms entreating them,
Jesus stood there and cried:
What moved the Lord? What inconceivable
Urgency of occasion stirred Him so?
Ah, quick the numbered days are stealing by;
They *will* not come to Him that they be saved!
And the Lord stood and cried:
Had He not told them of that Bread HE IS?
Had He not opened to their sealèd eyes
The mystery of that "Lamb" they brought to
God?

But nought perceived they; hardened they their
hearts;—
So the Lord stood and cried:
"Ho, every one that thirsteth," cried the Seer;
And that "last day" was water freely poured
By Israel, quick at symbols—now stone blind
To all of meaning by these signs conveyed:
Wherefore,—He stood and cried!

XXVII

Come unto Me and drink

If any thirst,—Come unto Me and drink!
I know your thirst and how ye seek to quench,—
This one with coins of gold—what help in these?
How can they plenish veins dried up and
  parched?
The blood is the life—what property hath gold
To mingle with the blood and feed the life?
  Come unto Me and drink!

The fiery draught of pleasure, this, would quaff—
"Behold, I drink, and shall be satisfied;
Come, fill the cup again, make strong the
  draught;
My thirst consumes me still, fill up, fill up;
Why niggard when thou pourest for me—life?"
Poor soul, he knows not death is in the cup,
  Nor comes to Me to drink.

A fiercer fever rages in the man
Whom lust of power consumes; arid his days;
Still higher place, more power, he fondly dreams,
Will cool parched lips, lay hand on burning eyes

Aflame with fever of consuming thirst:
What is in power that it should nourish life?
Come unto Me and drink!

A soul to love him—give him life for life—
This other craves, nor knows he shall not live
By draining another's cup to allay his thirst:
Waters unfed from higher source dry up;
The place grows pestilent—there's nought to drink:
See you, there's but one draught of life for all—
Come unto Me and drink!

What give I?—ask ye in your little faith,
Nor comprehend ye how a Man, in your midst,
Can stand and offer water to the world
That shall satisfy each individual thirst,
Shall send life coursing in full stream through the veins
Of any fainting soul who will rise and come—
Come unto Me and drink!

Scarce can ye comprehend that Life is one—
All lives of men replenished from one Source:
That he who comes not to the Source falls dry,
Is parched of fever, dried up in decay:
How can ye live save as from Me ye draw
That Water of Life I stand to offer you?
Come unto Me and drink!

XXVIII

They will, and will not, "come"

Come unto Me and drink! He stood and cried:
And every man perceived himself athirst;
Each saw as in a vision places green,
With sheltering trees fed by the Well of Life,
Fair fruits and shade and coolness in the heat:
As child makes sudden leap to reach his joy,
(Held fast in nurse's arm), so each man's soul
Sprang up within him, buoyant, towards that Well
Of living waters he beheld in Christ!
Not one there failed to apprehend the truth
As it fell from the Lord's lips. But that old Nurse—
Habit? Nature? How shall we call the crone?—
Held fast the struggling soul—"Nay, honey, still!
With all thy leaping, canst thou catch the moon?
Men travelling in the waste know well enough
This trick of the desert, to show watered spot
Which holds a hidden well; you come, there's nought!
So, whisht ye, child,—no water is for you,
But here be pretty baubles!"

"Come unto Me!
Prove thou the water real, drink of it:
'Tis delicious in the drinking, renovates;
The man who drinks goes able for his life,—
Treads wilderness ways with springing step, alert,
Nor knows the misery of pining drought:
And more; I show a mystery to you:—
That man who drinks shall be himself a well;
Out from him shall the living waters flow,
Yea, copious rivers, whereat many drink!
Come, then, and drink! if not for thine own thirst,—
Wouldst quicken desert places, faint souls lift?
Lovest thou not thy brethren? Is't nought to thee
That men be faint? Come, drink, and thou shalt save,
Shalt carry cooling waters where thou go'st:—
The Waters of Life may not be held in the cup
Of any one man's heart; they overflow,
Gather and spread and reach the furthest shore
Where thirsting wretches cower!"
This spake the Lord
Of the approaching day, when, all things done,
Finished on Calvary, the ascended Lord
Should pour the SPIRIT forth,—full stream of life
For the quickening of the nations.

XXIX

The thirsty came

A LAD was in the crowd, limp and athirst;
His hollow eyes were fixed on Him who spake:
Of all the words he'd heard, this was the first
Invited him, of life, to come and take:
Ne'er stepping from his place, he came and drank;—
Lo, Life was in the stream, pellucid, through him sank.

A weary man was there, who toiled to get,
With heavy labour, meat for his and him:
So dry he was, so flagging, all things let
And hindered the poor man; his eyes were dim
For very dearth of joy: he heard the word,
And came and drank that water offered of the Lord.

And there, an aged man,—ah, well might he,
Athirst through all his days, lie down and die,

Parched and unsatisfied; what hope might be
That he, old man, should drink and satisfy
That craving, long consumed him? "Come to Me!"
Saith One: unseen, he came, and filled his soul with glee.

And so they came, one here, another there,
A ghostly multitude whom no man saw:
Eager they haste and fearful; they would share
That water, Christ the Lord should gracious draw:
He gave them drink; none saw their lips to move,
Yet each who came went cool'd, sustained, fulfilled with love!

XXX

Two are athirst

(*The disciple*)

If any man in the world, at any time,
Be weary, feverish, exhausted, faint,
Through heavy wanderings in the horrid clime
The world affords its votaries—all attaint,—

Come unto Me, saith Christ to such an one,
Drink and be plenished with full life again
As when a child thou revelled'st: is there none
Holds cup to thee in all life's dreary plain?

Like the child Ishmael, wouldst lie down and
die?
Is nothing worth thy while, when every day
Repeats the last in dull monotony?
What ails thee then—hast thou no skill to say?

Two are athirst in this drought,—I, for thee;
And thou, not knowing, thirstest sore for Me!

XXXI

He thirsted first

FAINT with desire, thou hear'st the Master's cry:
Thy soul gets up and answers,—"I, too, thirst
For the living God! fulfil me or I die!"
And, lo, He comes with life!—He thirsted first;

Thy love, the draught He longed for; drink
then free
Of the fulness of God, nor fear thou canst ex-
haust:
Did all men lap at that stream there would be
Rivers of water still; no drop is lost!

But thou must *drink;* to know that water's there
Is not enough for any thirsting soul;
Drink, drink, thou fainting one! Come quick
and share
That Life which shall fill thee, as wert thou a
bowl!

That ONE should offer to *all* fainting souls
The sole cup which suffices and consoles!

XXXII

The multitude is divided

Must truth for aye be a dividing line
Separating men who share a common life,
Nay, chief friends, brothers sheltered by one roof?
Till now the pilgrims were unanimous,
(They from the country), friendly in desire
That He, this Rabbi, of good repute amongst men,
Should have fair dealing here in Jerusalem.

But that word, "Come unto Me," searched all men's hearts
With urgency of decision laid on each:
They might not rest in general good will
Towards any Rabbi who spoke words of truth,
This Man among the rest. The word went forth—
"Get up and come—choose this day whom ye serve!"
And, timorous, they held back. Some said, "Of a truth

This is the Prophet." Long had Israel held
Her house in readiness to welcome Him,
Sent of Jehovah, whom Moses had foretold:
The temerity of the men who recognised
In Christ that Prophet,—an avowal, made,
Which should enmity incur, nay, risk of life—
Moves admiration in these easier times:
A saint of latter days, wise Brother Lawrence,
Bids us distinguish,—"Whether is thine act
Of the understanding born or of the Will";
Here in this multitude, as in all crowds,
Were those who to their understanding leaned,
And those who embraced with *Will* the thing they knew.
The first, due weighing evidence, allowed.
"The Prophet, this": these others knew their soul
To rise in strong assurance, undismayed;
With solemn tones confess they,—"This is Christ!"
The multitude divide on that bold word;
On that side, those who would have light from without;
On this, those who by its light inherent know
The truth when they see it: these arise and "Come!"

Conviction of the mind is bitter-sure;
Vindictiveness is born of certainty:
Well so, it may be; how, otherwise, should men

Fight for that truth which to matter appertains
And hand on Science to the race to come?
But science is of the senses ascertained,
And there be realms where these no more convince;
Certainties, to be neither seen nor touched
Or judged by any signs men may perceive;
The man who knows on evidence is wroth,
In sudden hate, he turns on the thing put forth
With claims he is incompetent to weigh:
So, through a thousand years the Church has fared,
So, that day, suffered Jesus at their hands—
Those men who judged by evidence alone.

The amazing word has fallen in that crowd,—
"If any thirst, come unto Me and drink!"
One more hard saying,—powerful to divide
Chief friends, one family, a man's own heart!
And, lo, some of them would have taken Him—
Those who would fain be sure, demanded proof,—
Bitterly angry; how could that be true
Which by every sign they knew a witless lie?
They would have taken Him—the very men
Who had hung on His words but now! There stood the Lord,—
And none stretched hand to take, none rudely touched;
Did a screen ineffable—not seen of them—

Hedge round the Christ from sacrilegious touch
Until His time was come?
"This is the Christ,"—
Reiterated they who knew by signs
Infallible: "What, shall the Christ come forth
From Galilee?" the unbelieving cried,
Hot in the wrath of men who think they know
And hold their opponents liars, blind to truth:
"What make ye then of this, ye shameless ones,—
Hath not the Scripture said, 'Of David's seed,'
From out the village where great David was,
And shepherded his flock, shall come the Christ;—
Out of Bethlehem cometh He—Ye are possessed
With a lying spirit, ye ignorant and false!!"

XXXIII

"Never man spake as this Man"

MEANTIME, the Sanhedrin in session sate;
Had hasty summons called the Seventy
To confer on national emergency?
Fretful, in feverish anxiety,
They wait the return of the officers sent out
To apprehend this Man, the people's Seer:
What should they do with their prisoner? vexing
thought!
"An kill we Him, the Romans will accuse us
Of breaking their hateful laws." "Pooh, we can
deal
With subtlety—make these same Romans kill,
Act as our executioners—base part!—
And crucify this Jesus, for that He hath
Transgressed the laws of Rome—a thing to
prove:"
"A worthy scheme, subtle and simple, but how,
On what grounds, get conviction?"
While they spake,
The officers returned—crestfallen men—
No prisoner in their hand. "Why, where is He?

Why, Him, bring ye not hither?" How wonderful
The ways of God with men! These had gone forth,
Eager to gain blood-money; vindictive,
If but to justify their shameful part;
They'd watched and listened—hoped to catch a word,
Which should Jesus of Nazareth condemn: and lo,
The Truth rose up and, sudden, caught the men,
Shook them with violence till their naked soul
Stood fearful forth, and owned the Christ of God.

A wonder came to pass, a miracle!
These men, unknowing, had that act of Will
Performed, which turns a man; a "Sesame,"
Pronounced, imperious, by their sordid soul,
Had let in Christ—all lovely, all divine:
They saw and understood, and found grace—they!—
To speak the final word, unanswerable,
In every controversy concerning Christ:
No signs adduce they, mighty works performed,—
These had stirred wonder in the days gone by,
But now—what matter signs to them who know?
"Never man so spake"—they say, and, in that word,
Exhaust all argument, flout evidence!
Ye happy men, poor creatures of the Jews,
No theologian in all future years

Shall find the final word to say of Christ—
That word is yours for ever!
The angry Jews
Forgot that dignity of office, prized
Chief among their possessions, rose in wrath—
Hissed bitter words from out closed teeth, waved hands
To stress a scorn immeasurable; to these,
Their servants, spake as though to rulers born,
(Fierce wrath, like love, makes equal in a trice;)
Cried they, as to their fellows, "What, ye too,
Are ye also led astray, whose bread depends
On this august Assembly? Fie on you!
Poor ignorant fools, what better can ye know?
Look at your betters, hath any of them believed
On Him,—the Rulers or the Pharisees?
As rocks they stand—which He shall break upon!
Aye, as rocks they'll fall and crush Him!"
Was it so?
Or had the truth, a living stream, urged in
Through all obstructions,—flowing water's wont—
And were there amongst the Seventy (named "the Jews,"
As though the people counted not),—were there here
Parched souls that sighted water? God, He knows:
One such was moved to speak a timid word;—
On general principles would he take his stand;

None should suspect his anxiety to save
The Man his heart assured him was the Christ:
Had he not seen, that night they sent him
forth
To test this "interloper," a Presence there,
In that dim upper room, had come to abide
For ever with him, chiding?
Nicodemus saith—
"Doth our law judge a man except it hear
Him speak in his own defence?" Alas, for them,
The fearful advocates who would save a man
Nor compromise themselves! They fail to serve,
And bewray that they would hide. The Pharisees
In bitter spleen turned on him—"Art thou, too,
Of Galilee?" they hissed, and mouth'd at him,—
Opprobrious epithet then, as to-day,
Sure way to damn a cause! "Search thou and see—
No prophet cometh out of Galilee!"
Subtle their tactics,—name of scorn to fix
On them who followed Christ; who'd choose to be
Nicknamed a Galilean, in a land
Where purity of descent was more than life?
With curious pleasure note we, how disperse
The manifold charges made to prove that He,
Jesus of Nazareth, was not the Christ:
A single count remains: Of Galilee, He,

Whilst the Messias out of Judah comes:
Charge, got of ignorance on arrogance!
The Evangelist makes no comment; by their
    words,
Stand these condemned for ever.

XXXIV

The shameful woman

CHRIST sought the Mount of Olives, there to
pray;
While every man went on his homeward way
At the fall of night; the early morning found
The Lord again in the temple, and around,
Multitudes who had early come to hear;
He sat and taught the people.
To them, draw near
A group of the enemy, scribes and Pharisees,
Dragging a shameful woman. When she sees
The Lord, does her vileness stab her dagger-wise,
That wretched creature—centre of all eyes?
All eyes but His—The Lord averts His face—
Sure, punishment enough for one so base!
They clamour,—"Moses bade stone such an
one,
But what say'st Thou,—see'st any way to
atone?"
Now, they had caught Him in a trap, egress
At either end of which should Him confess
Traitor to th' Law, or, in complicity
With one whose odious vice might find no plea:

Photo, Alinari *Marconi*

THE WOMAN TAKEN IN ADULTERY

But Jesus, stooping down, wrote on the ground,
With His finger curious characters performed:
They will not take His silence for reply;
Reproof is lost on them: in vain they ply
The Lord with unseemly questions: He arose,
And fell the lightning of His glance on those,
The shameless Pharisees, had brought her there;
Then came the Lord to judgment: "Who is aware
Of no sin in this kind, now let him cast
The first stone at the woman:" forth they passed,
Shamed, and in silence as a shadow steals;—
Yon old man reverend in his turn feels
The shame he'd cast on the sinner ta'en in sin,
Loathsome, but shared by every man within
That circle of accusers; see them go—
Unmeet to face Him, who all hearts doth know.

The woman in the midst nor dared to move,
Nor dared regard the Lord of holy love;
And Jesus, looking round, said, "Where are they
Who accused thee, woman? hath no man cast a stone?"
"No man, O Lord!" "Then will I not alone
Condemn thee; go, and henceforth sin no more:"—
Was the Lord's word all-potent to restore?

We are not sure; we know not if, indeed,
They brought to Christ that shameful broken
reed;
We know not if the Lord stooped down and
wrote:
Did He, in truth? Quite other ways, we note,
Majestic, simple, in the Lord who knows
To speak the word He means; nor deigns to
pose,
Nor by effect dramatic catch the crowd.
A holy legend doubtless, and allowed
A place within the Volume for the sake
Of that it teaches; a parable, to make
Men pause shamefast, and know such sin is theirs,
E'en more than the woman's: that there's One
who cares
For the veriest drabbled soul betrayed to sin,
And knows to discriminate.

BOOK IV

THE LIGHT OF THE WORLD

(The Great Controversy)

XXXV

Let there be light

Let there be light! came forth the Almighty Word:
And, lo, the sun a flood of radiance poured
On that vast chaos, dim, unlovely, dank:
As when a Queen goes forth, each in his rank,
Her subjects place them, waiting on her smile,—
So Order rose from Chaos that, erewhile,
Occupied the waste places: Life came out
To choose her habitation, upon the rout
Of those disordered forces cast pell-mell about.

Light waved his potent wand and all the fields
Are, sudden, green and lovely: horror yields
His place to Beauty—who the Light can split
Into rays of colour such as shall befit
For painting flowers, of birds, the plumage gay,
The heavens themselves, adorned for break of day.

The world made fair, lo, Joy and Hope come forth
To bask them in the Beauty gave them birth;
And every little bird shouteth aloud for mirth.

Warmth followed in the Light, and soft caressed
The new-born things Life cherished at her breast:
Like maiden blushing 'neath her lover's eye,
The new Earth glowed before the majesty
Of the Sun in the sky emitting Warmth and Light—
Dispelling fearful terrors of old Night,
So long had reigned and held the earth in thrall:—
The flowers put on their beauty; young lambs call;
Lo, Hope and Love and Gladness dominate them all.
"We have the Sun for ever!" was the song
Created things uplifted: but, ere long,
The Light, the glorious Light, began to fade;
The lovely valleys sank in ominous shade;
Anon, the hill-tops lost their roseate glow;
Violets and roses red quick ceased to shew
Their tinting exquisite; the lilies white—
Pure chalices to hold distillèd light—
With all the beauteous flowers, turn black in awful night.

And all Light's train of presences divine,
Extinguished by fell darkness, cease to shine;
Beauty goes hide herself; Order retires;
Hope, Love and Joy let out their genial fires:
Foul vapours of the night enwrap the scene
But yesterday had all so radiant been:
And all the creatures know that all their bliss
Proceedeth from the Sun's transcendant kiss;
The Sun removed, ah me, their state is all amiss!

XXXVI

The people sat in darkness

THE people sat in darkness; none could read
Directions for the way, or see to go:
"Nay, whither go we?" "Whence do we proceed?"
Anxious, they queried sad in accents low:

Their Seers strained dim eyes to penetrate
The heavy darkness, closed on every side:
"What news then bring ye?" cried those desolate,
"The gods, what angers them that they deride

Our impotence, our misery's extreme?"
Sad poets made reply with *Œdipus*,
And other tales, each lurid as bad dream,—
As nightmare where no succour is for us,

No issue from our ills: but one or two
Strong spirits pierced the darkness well-nigh through.

Holman Hunt

THE LIGHT OF THE WORLD

By permission of The Autotype Fine Art Co. Ltd.,
74 New Oxford Street, London, W.C.

XXXVII

"I am the Light"

Lo, One stood up and cried, I AM THE LIGHT
OF ALL THE WORLD! A sudden lightness spread—
In each man's heart a gleam of light was shed,
A moment's sweet emergence from the night.

The blessedness of light! With brows grown bright,
Some basked in emanations of the Day,
Allowed the blessed light its generous play,
Nor feared the radiance should take instant flight,—

An evanescent joy: on these He shone,
The Dayspring from on high with healing come
For all men's miseries: but there were some,
Enwrapped them in the darkness; would have none
Of the gifts He came dispensing, chose to roam
Groping in darkness—mocking at the SUN!

XXXVIII

In the Light

(The disciple)

"How fair thou art, O soul! how still a grace
Mantles thy face!
What pure cool chambers do thine eyes reveal!
Sure dwells in thee some luminous mystery?"
"As yon dull orb that yet so shines to thee,
I do but stand
In the Light."

"What seest thou, O soul, where thou dost stand?"
"A shifting sand
Where vile things stir and live—pride, envy, strife,
Malice and anger, all that prey on love—
Lo, these within me doth the Light reprove!
Yet fain I stand
In the Light."

"O soul, poor soul, how bearest thou such sight?
How sad a plight!"

"Aye, sad, but there is help beside the pain;
Help in a word; I do but say to One,
'Lord, I am vile!' and, lo, the ill is gone!—
Blameless I stand
In the Light."

"Seest thou no more?" "I see a foe who stands
With ordered bands
Surrounding me; and from his hand each hurls
A dart to wound." "Poor soul, how 'scapest thou?"
"One bears a shield: no scathe shall He allow
To reach who stand
In the Light."

"This the whole cheer, poor soul, light brings to Thee?"
"Nay, *One* I see—
In heaven, in earth, but One: none may rehearse,
Nor any comprehend save them who see,
The healing of the Vision: He shines on me;—
Wherefore I stand
In the Light!"

"Hast any more to tell?" "I see the way,
The devious way
My feet must tread, mark'd out all fair for me;

A path I ne'er had found, nor finding, kept,
Save for the Day: in the past night I slept;
But now walk on,
In the Light.

"And more: I see all souls about me shine:
In Light divine,
Fair do they glow; the Light doth shine on all,
Though not all know; and, ah, this heart would throw
The arms of brotherhood round all, that so,
Assured, we stand
In the Light!"

"O soul, help me! I, too, would feel His beam,
But, ah, I seem
Too vile to meet the Day!" "Brother, e'en now,
He shines on thee: thy very fear doth prove
The darkness vanish'd; who confess and love,
Are they who stand
In the Light!"

XXXIX

Whence and Whither

Turning to them who followed, Christ declared:—
"The man that follows Me, he shall have light"—
Not his, to grope and stumble in the way;
Buoyant his steps, for, seeing, he doth walk
In the Light that is Life also; he is strong.

How mighty is the Truth!
The Pharisees heard this utterance, nor denied;
Said not, "The Man's a fool, or, doth blaspheme!"—
As we should say to one who dared proclaim
Himself the source whence emanates all light:—
But not if we had heard, and knew them true,
Those words stupendous, making as nought the sum
Of all words uttered by men anywhere:
Haply we'd cried, "Arise and shine, O Sun!"

Not thus, these proud men, keen, of legal mind;
Their tongues refused them to deny the Light:
But was there no side way t' oppose, condemn?

They have it:—"Saith the Law, Who witnesseth
To his own merits, boasts the powers he hath,
His witness is not true!" (so, long ago
Had Christ Himself declared; out of His mouth,
Would they convict Messias).

"Nay, ye do err;
One only among men may Himself proclaim;
Needs must He tell what He knows, for none
besides,
Born into the world in the past, none yet to come,
Save One, can answer you those queries fateful,
Insistent at the door of all men's hearts,—
'Whence come I? Whither go?' Alone among
men,
I know whence I came forth, and whither go:
Ye know not; wherefore needs must I reveal
What the flesh, and that dim understanding,
aids
The conclusions of the flesh, cannot attain.
After the flesh ye judge Me; ye are sure;
I judge not you or any man,—not yet;
But if I judge, My judgment must be true;
I judge in the light of truth—how shall I err?
And every judgment rising in My thought
Is that of Two agreed: the Father, He
Is with Me in those secret places where
The thoughts of men are formed; and not alone
I testify; Where I am, is the Father:
The claim ye make, that two voices shall attest,

Is met as never in the courts of men;
I witness of Myself—Who am the Truth,
And the Father adds His witness to the Son's:
Did ye but know, how would ye shrink abash'd
Before these awful WITNESSES at your Bar!"

An instant were they shamed; then, impudent,
They made mouths at Him, stretching out their
necks,—
"Thy Father, and Thy Father! what vain talk!
But where's Thy Father, this we fain would
know?"
And Jesus, infinite in patience, said:—
"To know is to perceive, to comprehend;
Ye know not Me, who stand in your midst; how,
then,
Shall ye know the Father, never seen of men
Save as He is revealed to them who love?
Knew ye Me, then the Father would ye know."
These words spake Jesus in the treasury
The while He taught in the temple. Never
man
In that so hostile multitude laid hands
On the Christ, for all their bravery: withheld
By means inscrutable, they bide their time;
His hour was not yet come.

XL

Who art Thou?

HE spake again: "Behold, I go away;
And ye who drive Me hence shall seek in vain
For Him who came to save you; too late, when
Your hour, now running its last sands, hath passed;
And ye shall die in your sin,—whose magnitude
Would send you, stricken with dismay, from
hence
To self-immolation, saw ye but the truth!
But ye are blind; having eyes, ye see not;
And where I go, there is no place for you;
What place for you in the full light of God
Where Truth alone survives? Outcast, ye go,
Lost souls in desolate wastes where I am not."

Awed and yet obdurate, the Jews cried out,—
"What threat is this to mock us? Where goes
He?
Will He kill Himself to accomplish these brave
words—
'Where I go, come not ye; ye cannot come'?"
So, sneering, spake they, half to convince the
crowd,

And half themselves to assure.
Again, He spake,
(His patience as an ocean never drained),—
"See you, there be two worlds; ye are from beneath,
Of this low world where lies are ta'en for truth,
And men receive not truth because they *will*
Not to receive those things of the world above.
I am from above, but ye are of this world:
Can fire and water mingle nor destroy
The one, the other? Me, ye seek to kill,
And ye, ye shall die in your sins, slain of the truth:
Poor souls, have pity on your own lost state!
Behold, a door of escape I still hold ope
For him who will see the truth: e'en as I speak,
Uneasy thoughts stir in your breast; ye know;
Feeble conviction is pleading to be heard,
And fear assails: Come, listen, not to Me,
But to inner voices uttering fearful things!
At the eleventh hour of the day, I bid—Believe
That I am He of Israel's hopes and fears—
The Promise treasured for these thousand years!
I know ye *can* believe, and *will* ye now,
At the last hour, believe, that I may save?
Else, die ye in your sins!"
At this dread word,
Terror gat hold of them: husky, they cried,
From out parched lips,—"Who art Thou, then, declare?"

"Ask ye Me now?" said the Lord; "these many times
And from the beginning have I not announced
That I and the Father are One; that I am He
Of whom your Law and your prophets testify?
Ye think to be rid of Me—that, at your hands,
The Son of Man shall die; nay, that, at the worst,
E'en should ye die yourselves, there were an end:—

"Ye foolish people and unwise, not thus
Doth Life make end! I have many things to speak
And to judge concerning you: this controversy,
Ye think to close with death, shall still go on:
But on that day ye stand before the Judge,
Lo, He shall speak; not ye. Ye shall discern,
By the Light, which to-day ye will not choose to see,
Blinding your eyes, the King ye would not serve;
Th' inexorable Judge, who, for He must,
Pronounceth sentence: first, will He rehearse
The thoughts that give complexion to your lives,
The arrogance and hate, the greed and lust,
That blind your eyes to the truth: for ye know well
What treason ye would compass: none can hear
The voice of the Son of Man nor be convinced;

Photo, J. Caswall Smith *Burne-Jones*

DIES DOMINI

And well ye know that treason's in your hearts—
That ye seek the life of your King, the Coming
One,
Knowing that in His realm is no place for you,
For wrong and rapine wrought on these poor
folk
Whom ye would rob of their God. Away with
you!

"And other things shall ye hear when ye pass the
bounds
Of that ye call your life: the words I speak,
Each word of Mine that hath reached you by
report—
Or you have heard direct—shall sound in your
ears,
For ever, without pause. Before the Judge,
Shall ye take your stand, nor ever leave the dock,
But always shall ye hear those many things
I have to speak concerning you."

XLI

"I have many things to speak and to judge concerning you"

(*The disciple*)

WITH me, hast Thou a controversy, Lord?
Hast many things to say concerning me?
Must I stand prisoner, catechised by Thee—
Is this the import of Thine awful word?

Wouldst know how I have treated all those
friends—
Scattered like flowers along my way of life—
This, slighted, this one injured, this, in strife,
Hurt by my hard pursuing of mine ends?

Wouldst Thou inquire of those words I've
heard,
Still waking morn by morn my callous ear,—
Cold to Thy counsels, all too quick to hear
Unseemly words;—seldom by Thee deterr'd!

Good Lord, come now in judgment—*now* draw
near;
Ere the last Day, speak Thou,—and make me
hear!

XLII

The Lord pleads with the Jews

"But how shall I convince you? How compel
  Your blind eyes to perceive that He is true
  Who in His love and pity sent to you
His Son beloved, Ambassador, to tell

"Those things the Father whispered in His ear:
  These have I from the housetop cried aloud,
  All have imparted to the witless crowd,
For haply some might, understanding, hear."

So spake the Lord, but no man yet perceived
  That of the Father spake He; none was sure
  What those things signified He should endure;
Their minds were stirred, but not yet they believed.

Cried the Christ then;—"When ye have lifted up
  The Son of Man, too late shall ye perceive
  The truth of Him whom ye will not believe,—
When I have drained for you the bitter cup,

"My Father giveth Me: for not alone
Am I in aught I say, or aught I do:
Not wilful, would I My own thought pursue,
But, as God bids Me, would I men atone

"With the solicitous Majesty on high;
I do the things that please Him; hear ye, then;
Let Me not spend in vain on stubborn men
The very words of God: hear, lest ye die!"

Thus pleaded Christ in passionate urgency
With the men He had come to save; and some were moved;
Yea, many believed on Him, who men so loved—
"I am content," saith He, "for them to die."

XLII

To the Jews who believed

TENDER, Christ turned to the relenting Jews,—
The very priests and Pharisees, His foes,
Who from the crowd of His enemies came forth
And gave up all to take their part with Him :—

"Well have ye done to come, ye happy men,
Moved by the words I spake ; now, seize the truth,
For words are evanescent, quick disperse,
Invisible vapour, in the scorching heat
Of fiery persecution : wherefore abide—
Come in and out as to a dwelling safe—
Abide in the words I speak ; turn errant thoughts
And fearful back into that hiding place,
The words which I have said ; so are ye safe,
Tho' ye should follow all the way I tread
To prison and to judgment ; ye shall know
The truth, nor fear at all ; ye shall be free—
In prison cell as on the broad highway."

But they were new disciples, scarce had conn'd
The first syllable of that new lore He taught,

And though they loved Him, they were wroth
with Him :—
"What's this," they cried, "of freedom ?
Abraham's seed
Are we, and ne'er have been in bondage, we,
To any man : what means, 'ye shall be free'?"
And all the Jews cried, turbulent, "We are
free!"
And, "We are free!" the people shouted loud,
Vociferous, till hoarse was every throat.

Christ in His godlike patience, once again,
Began from the beginning : might they know
That this their body was not all of them ;
That their spirit loved and hated, sorrow'd,
joy'd,—
Then would they learn that the bondsman is not
caged
In stone and iron ; that fetters hang, con-
cealed
From the casual eye—nay, worn with easy
grace ;
And many a prisoner tied and bound goes free
To his own thinking and in the eyes of men.
"For," saith the Lord, "one fetter only binds
The bodies and souls of men ; who committeth sin,
He is the slave of sin, nor can escape
By labours of his hands, by sweat of brow :
Ye call yourselves free ;—the Roman in the land,
And in sin's fetters, are ye free indeed ?

E'en in your sins think ye t' inherit the earth,
Grow rich and prosper on spoil of subtle wits?
Brief is your day as that of the pampered slave
Who rejoices in his bonds, for he's at ease,
And dwells secure in plenty. Comes a day,
His master takes offence and casts him out:
Only the son is safe; the house is his;
And none can drive him forth. But should the son,
Inheriting, take pity on those slaves
And set them free, they shall be free indeed,—
Shall no more hang on the fickle nod of him
Who owns and may abuse them.
Such are ye;
'The children of Abraham,' say ye, therefore free?
Nay, yours, a bondage Abraham never knew;—
Know ye not then the law, 'Who sheds man's blood,
By man shall his blood be shed'? Ye are not free,
Ye're still in bonds, who ponder murderous thoughts;
These drive you and compel to murderous deed;
How are ye free, as slave-gang, driven by sin?
Ye cannot help yourselves; ye needs must sin;
Your father sees to 't that ye do his work,
An ye will not give My words free course in you:
The things I speak, I have with My Father seen;
And ye—fulfil your father's mandate well!"

XLIV

The Jews and the LORD

The Jews. Abraham is our father!
THE LORD. Abraham went
From Chaldee where he prospered, for he heard
The word of God which bade him. Lo, I come
To bid you forth from where men sit at ease
And take their wage of sin. Rise up, come forth;
Behave as Abraham's seed, and quit the place
Where sinners be; so shall ye do, indeed,
The works of Abraham who knew to obey the word:
Do ye with ardent welcome treasure up
My words, God's message to you? As a viper stings
The hand that feeds and cherishes, ye turn:
I offer words which shall manumit bond-slaves,—
And ye go about to kill Me. Whose are ye?
Whose seed is a murderous brood? Not Abraham's, sure
Instant obeyed he the word. *Your* father's hests,
As faithful, ye fulfil.

The Jews. Not born of adult'rous bed,
The Jewish nation ; a higher lineage yet
Than descent from Abraham claim we ; we are
God's ;
Our Father's He who Abraham called forth,
For He had a favour to us : one Father ours,
Even God Himself!

THE LORD. Shall not a man then love
His father ? Shall he not perceive, quick-eyed,
His father's image, loving that he sees ?
Were God your father, then would ye love Me ;
His image and superscription would ye find
Writ in Mine aspect ; in My words, His voice
Would ye discern with ready filial ear ;
For He sent Me to you ; I come not of Myself ;
Out from the Father came I, begotten Son.

The Jews. What means this talk ? We fail to
understand !

THE LORD. Aye, and why fail ye ? Hath
none ever tried
The effect of reasoned speech on stone-deaf ears ?
The deaf man sees lips move, but hears no
sound ;
E'en so are ye, for one hath sealed your ears ;
Your father the devil seals them lest ye hear
And be convert and live.

The Jews. Why molest us then ?
Out of Thy mouth we judge Thee ; the devil
seals
The ears Thou wouldst address, so sayest Thou ;

What help then? Where's the good?
THE LORD. It is your will
To do the lusts of your father—hate and lie
And kill Me for those words which should save; wherefore,
Ye cannot hear; a man is ruled by him
Whom he wills to serve: and service have ye ta'en
With him, the devil.
The Jews. What of him? We fain would know;
Welcome to duteous son his father's praise,
And Thou say'st we are his children!
THE LORD. Hear ye then;
In the son's lineaments men the father trace:
A murderer from the beginning was your sire,—
And you, his seed, lie in secret wait to kill
A Man who has done nor spoken aught but good:
Are ye not then his children? A liar, he;
From the beginning, could not endure the truth,
Nor keep his place where truth is all in all,
And none conceives a lie; how could he bear
The bewildering light of truth? Who hears the truth,
Must have inherent fitness—truth in him,
To act, prehensile, on the truth he hears:
Thus furnished, are men born; who wills a lie,
Loses the truth that is in him: thus did he;
When he speaks a lie, he speaketh of his own;

And every lie men think is begotten of him,
For he is a liar and the father of lies.

The Jews. Aye, but what's that to us? We've said no lie!

THE LORD. No lie, and ye seek My life! Who proveth, then,
That in aught I have done amiss? Benighted souls,
Who will not bear the Light, perceive ye not
That a liar has no power to hear the truth,—
Incessant in your ears. Why not believe,
When I tell you all the truth? Ye are not of God,
Are no true sons of Him who is the Truth.
Ye have another father, him, to whom lies
Are as his meat and drink; he needs must lie;
And ye, take ye not after him?

XLV

What is truth?

(*The disciple*)

NAY, what is truth? the cynic lightly cried;
But not to him the Incarnate Truth replied:
Who sees the light must have an eye;
Who music hears must bring an ear;
The seeing may things fair espy;
To the hearing, harmonies appear:
Who truth discerneth, he too hath a test,
A talisman of virtue in his breast.

Truth lieth not in this or that true thing
Careful observed;—plumage on insect's wing:
Nor in exact report, of how—
This curious thing one saw in the street;
That behaviour he was seen to allow,—
Conduct in such a man unmeet!
These instances be true; but truth is more
Than a man hears with his ears, or any lore

Careful collects he with observant eye
From Nature's book, right-full of mystery;

Or gathers from the written page
Where men record with duteous pains
Things which transpire from age to age,
Reckoning their losses up and gains:
We praise men as they garner what is true;
But the Truth—find they not thus, nor thus pursue.

For Truth is as the sun and lights up all
The shows of earth,—its treasures great and small;
And men, distract, see trifling things
Show radiant in the dazzling light
The sun on any object flings
Presented to the gazer's sight:
Lo, here the Truth! the man enraptured cries,—
On worthless gewgaw fixed, his gloating eyes.

But, who would see the Truth, the Sun must see,
Nor be contented by his light to trace
Glories of colour here and there;—
"Sufficient," saith he, "for my sight;
I am too weak, I cannot bear
The effulgence of immediate light."
So he pieces shining bits that light to make
Which shows his faltering steps the way to take!

But, see, the Truth is undivided, whole;
Presented instant to the timorous soul;
Foolish, she hangs back in dismay,
Would fain content her with a part,
Nor knows she hath the gift to essay
All produce offered at her mart:
For lack of will to choose the Infinite,
She closes on poor bargains,—sorry wight!

Ah, happy man who sees the Pearl of Truth!
He tries it by due test in very sooth,—
But, an you ask him how he knows,
No answer hath he ready,—cries,
"Look, look, how radiance from it flows,
That Pearl of Truth, to please all eyes!"
As though that simple man would say, "The light
Is its own evidence for men with sight!"

XLVI

The controversy (continued)

THE LORD. Nay, ye that hear the truth nor yet believe,
Know ye not, truth must needs compel a man
To know, for truth is mighty.—How is it, then,
Ye hear the truth and deny? A mystery's here:
He that is of God heareth the words of God,
And all the words of God be very truth,
And every word of truth is a word of God;
Truth is the language common to all souls
Who are of God: they hear and must believe:
But ye believe not for ye are not of God:
Truth is as home-bred speech to foreign ear
To you who 've not grown up by the Father's hearth,
Accustomed to that language of the home:
To you, 'tis senseless gabble.

The Jews. A Samaritan
Art Thou and hast a devil! Said we not well
In that? How else couldst reckon us aliens,
Us, the Jews—God's chosen?

THE LORD. I have not a devil,
But I speak the truth to ears that cannot hear;

I honour the Father, and ye dishonour Me
Who come forth from the Father—Son of His love;
But let that be; My glory seek not I:
Mine honour is with the Father,—He shall judge;
But, O ye Jews, fall ye not into the hands
Of the living God for judgment! Take ye thought
Ere final doom against you be pronounced!
There is a way of escape: keep ye My word,
And, lo, e'en death shall you pass by unhurt;
He never shall see death who keeps My word!

(*A timid soul crept up:* "Lord, what is 'keep'?
How shall we keep Thy word as 'twere a thing,
A jewel in a casket?" *And the Lord,*—
"As jewel keep it, ponder, love to look,
Take it and gaze on it as dear to thee,—
The word thou cherishest: so thou shalt live,
Nor ever taste of death." *Then, that poor soul;*—
"What then is 'death,' good Lord? I know amiss:"
"Aye, Death is when the soul goes out from God;
The soul's and body's parting, that is nought!")

XLVII

Abraham is dead

A Jew. Why, here, a madman, devil-possessed
in sooth;
Who ever heard of a man that did not die?
Our history's crammed with marvels wrought of
God
Through this or that, his servant: but that a
man
Should live and live through each succeeding
age,—
Ha, ha, a fool's dream, arrogant! Abraham,
Himself, the Father of us all, is dead,
And Moses and Elias,—the mighty roll
Of the prophets, dead be they! And here is one,
A Man of no account, presumes to say
That if one keep His word he shall not die,—
Nay, he shall never die through all time's years!
Pray, who art Thou that swellest there in pride?
Abraham is dead—art more than Abraham?
The prophets, they be dead, and shalt Thou live,
And Thy followers, shall they, too, ever live?
Whom makest Thou Thyself? Fool's prate is this,
Child's wonder-tale, unseemly for grown men.

THE LORD. Ye think to belittle Me with scornful speech;
But, see you, slighting words reach not the Man
Who is unsolicitous of any praise,
Credit, renown or glory men can give.
Blame and reproach pass such an one unhurt:—
The glory which is Mine ye cannot touch;
No words may vilify, no deeds detract,
From glory the Father sheddeth on His Son!

(Did some one in the crowd with open eyes
Perceive a halo of glory round the Son,
Encircling Him, luminous, and—separate?)

Ye men, why will ye lie? Ye hear the Truth,
Nor know it for the Truth, but question, scoff,
Prove it impossible by all your tests,
Impossible—therefore, false; to call the Truth
A lie, is the most damning of all lies
The father of lies can foist on credulous men:
Nay, seek to comprehend—hear and be saved!

XLVIII

Christ's solicitude for the Jews

As eager mother runs to save her child
On the verge of a precipice,
As labouring swimmer struggles toward the man
Quick sinking in the flood,
As men who fight with fire face the flames
Urgent to save some wretch;—
So laboured the Lord with urgency divine
To reach those callous Jews;
Would they but hear, would they but understand!
Might no ray penetrate
The thick intellectual darkness that hemmed in,—
Enclosed them as a shroud
Of many cerements closely overlaid?
Knowing the might of truth,
That every man must recognise the truth
He hears, in his own despite;—
Christ toiled incessant through the days of the Feast
To convince those obdurate Jews:
The coverings that enwrapp'd them, one by one,
He took and stripped away,—

That they be cold? Nay, that the light should
come,
That truth might penetrate:
Their law, religion, pride of race, were torn
From shivering backs to lure
Cold wretches to the glow of light divine:
They snatched their rags again,—
Those wrappings of the dead that held them
swathed:
Christ cries in vain to them;
The words of the Master fall on insensate ears
And are no more perceived
Than high seas, breaking on the obdurate cliff,
Than ardent sunshine spent on prison walls!

XLIX

"I beseech Thee, shew me Thy glory"

Lord, what is glory? ask we in distress,
Our eyes on the Son of Man, afflicted sore,
Yet speaking of "the Father" evermore,
And of that glory out of nothingness

The Father, who alone hath power to bless,
Upon the anointed Son doth constant pour:
And, What is glory? ask we, and confess
That ignorance we cherish and deplore.

"Shew me Thy glory, Lord!" Thy servant cried;
Thy goodness was Thine answer,—made to pass
Before the Prophet's eyes: and, satisfied,
That one man saw Thy glory as in a glass:

Was it the Christ he saw, sore suffering,
So might He to mankind salvation bring?

L

"Our glory must we shew"

Our glory's nought when we ourselves do praise:
The Christ praised not Himself, nor glorified,
But, lowly, stood He there,—the Ancient of Days,
Whose splendour sudden shewn had deified

Him straight before those Jews who rude denied:
Had they once seen Him shine out glorious,
Messias, going forth victorious,
How would they shame them that they had decried!

'Tis the old tale; our glory must we shew,
Display fine things we own, good deeds we do;
Such great ones, we, our praises needs must flow
From the gaping mouths of all the idle crew:

We will not rest us quiet in that shade
For modest souls which our Redeemer made!

LI

What is glory?

THE LORD. Verily, verily, who keeps My word,
That man shall not see death.
The Jews. Abraham is dead,
The prophets are dead; art greater than
Abraham?
Who art Thou then? Whom makest Thou Thyself?
THE LORD. I seek not Mine own glory; did
I so,
I were as foolish men who plumage preen
To spread before th' admiring multitude:
This do they, ignorant of what glory is,
That he who wears it knows not he's adorned
Of God, who alone gives honour. Ye see not
The glory of goodness shining from a man:
This radiance gives My Father; and on Me,
Unstinted, pours the glory which is His,—
Author of goodness, glorious in His love!
Him, name ye your God the while ye know
Him not
Nor can discern; else knew ye Me likewise;
I know Him; nay, ne'er mutter "blasphemy!"

Should I deny that I know Him, then, like you,
I were a liar: for whoso knows the truth
May not deny.
I keep My Father's word,
Enduring contradiction, as Roman guard
Holds fast the imperial standard, dies for it.
The Jews. What is this word Thou keep'st?
THE LORD. Your Scriptures shew,
Your prophets testify; Abraham himself,—
Was it for nought he left the Chaldean plains
And went, a homeless wanderer? He was glad;
His wand'rings, losses, famine, sword, nay, death,
Were as nought to Abraham, for he saw My day,
Lived in the fulness of the coming time,
And rejoiced in God his Saviour.
The Jews. What stuff is this!
Thou'rt not yet fifty years old, and hast Thou seen
Abraham, our father?
(His countenance was marred
More than the sons of men with lines of grief;
What havoc had been wrought that men conceived
Him old—past the prime of life! Behold, and see
The Man of Sorrows! tear-channelled, see, His cheek,
Deep lines of suffering round His eyes, His mouth!
"Not fifty yet," they say,—"but looking more."
What iron pen had, cruel, chiselled grooves
On the brow august of Him whom we adore!)

THE LORD. Before Abraham was, I AM. Ere God had laid
The foundations of the world, lo, I was there
In council with the Father. No prophet spake
But as I gave him words: no patriarch
Walked humbly with his God and gave their meat
To children and children's children, but I was there
Sustaining that good man in righteous ways.

The Jews. Hear Him, ye people, hear! What blasphemies
Pour from His tongue—a black Gehenna flood!

And they took up stones to cast at Him; but now,
He was not there; in instant's space He was gone:
In vain they searched the temple's corridors,
Peeped behind hundred pillars, peered in doors,—
The Lord was not in the temple. Had He gone—
"Ephraim is joined to his idols, let him be,"—
Was this the sentence His withdrawal spake?

LII

Before Abraham was, I AM

ALWAYS, O Christ, wert there? At the cool of eve
Didst walk in the Garden with the primal pair?
When Enoch mounted chariot, wert Thou there?
Did old Methuselah see Thee and believe?

Didst watch with David, hastening to retrieve
Thy chosen Singer, that he yet might share
Divine Companionship, might still declare
All that a man may of his God conceive?

Did Plato know Thee in the dim obscure?
Great Alexander, saw he Righteousness,
A world his mighty arm was made to bless?
Was Phidias of Thy Beauty very sure?

In every age, where man at goodness wrought,
Lord, wert Thou with him, unperceived, unsought?

LIII

Did this man sin?

Now, as the Lord passed forth, a man He saw,
Blind from his birth: and the disciples draw
Close to their Lord to ask Him, inly vexed,
Of a matter which had troubled and perplexed
Their hearts for many a day: now, they would
know;—
For sure, their part, the ways of God to shew.

"Master, who then hath sinned, this man or
they
Who him begat, that blind, he treads his
way?"—

No new thing to suppose the drunkard's child
Needs must his parent follow; that the wild
And lawless vagabond who runs the street
Must children bear for gracious ways unmeet;
Or that the sufferer must look within—
His punishment bewrays his secret sin:
Hard judgments, these, from man's embittered
heart;
But Christ declares the merciful true part.

"This man hath done no sin to mark him worse
Than other men—one labouring under curse,—
Nor have the man's parents sinnéd in such wise;
What think ye? there be men the Father tries
With utmost suffering, that they honoured be
To manifest God's power. For who hath eyes to
see,
The works of God are manifest in strange ways;
To work His works,—the business of men's days.
'Sore suffering,' say ye, 'is that work divine,
Enduring much, make we God's glory shine
Effulgent before men? But God is good,
And pities men.' Ye have not understood;
One labours and one suffers, which is best?
Nay, go and do God's will; leave ye the rest:
Not suffering and not doing is man's part,
But, to discern God's will—the single art,
A man must exercise whilst it is day;
When the night cometh none may see the way.
And night approacheth, when no man can work,—
When earth and heaven be wrapped in darkness
murk:
I am the Light of the world whilst I am here;
Who walks with Me, to that man shall appear
The Will of God—to suffer or perform;
And, doing God's will, nought shall that man harm.
But the hour when I depart is close at hand;
Behoves ye straight to keep your Lord's command."
"But, Lord, if Thou go hence, how shall we see?
Reft of Thy light, in darkness shall we be!"

LIV

The man receives sight

AND as they spake, the blind man heard;
Thoughts unaccustomed rose and stirred
Within that darkened room, his mind;—
Of light, of work, of how to find
The Man who owned that gracious voice
Which moved him to make glad, rejoice
That, not for sin, his God had dealt
The misery he erst had felt
Shut him from out that smile of God
Which glorifies the very sod.

Now steps draw near; a tender touch
Falls upon him had suffered much;
A coolness laid on the poor eyes
Soothes him to peace; but, hark,—"Arise,
Go wash thee in Siloam's pool."
He dipped his face in waters cool;
The clay removed, he lifted eyes;
Beauty and light, supreme surprise,
Were for the man who had never seen:
For the first time, the leaves were green,

(How often had he felt their sheen!)
For the first time, the winds made play
With dancing shadows in the way:
The children gazed, and flitted by,—
At last he saw life's pageantry
Who had sat as blindfold at a play,
Scarce heeding what the actors say.

As mother seeking child she's lost,
Small heed had he for sights that crossed
His eyes, amazed: where then was HE
Had taught his stone-blind eyes to see?
Scarce guided by his new found sense
He finds the temple; (how immense!)
There he the tones he knew might hear,
And see that Face had grown so dear
As imaged in his curtained mind;—
"O that I knew where I might find!"

The folk observed him seek about;
Some strangeness in him roused their doubt;
He went not with the accustomed ease,
Familiar, of the man who sees:
Neighbours were there who knew the man;
With eyes brought close his face to scan,—
"Sure this is he who begged for alms,
(Extracted oft from grudging palms!)"
"Nay, but that beggar's image, he,"
Said others, "but this man can see."
"I am the man,"—the beggar said;

And all the folk, astonishéd,
Cried, "Who hath ope'd thine eyes then,
say,
That thou goest seeing on thy way?"
As one intones a holy song
Then took he up his tale—not long:—
"The man named Jesus, He made clay,
Anointed mine eyes, nor let me stay,
But bade me to Siloam go
And wash; I see;—no more I know."
"Where is He?" cried the impatient crowd;
"I know not," said the man aloud,
But cried he ever in his mind,—
"O that I knew where I might find!"

They bring him to the Pharisees—
This marvel, one born blind who sees;
Now it was on the Sabbath day
That Jesus, merciful, made clay;
"How gottest thou thy sight?" they cry;
"He put clay on mine eyes, and I
Washed, and do see." "Who Sabbath keeps,
Nor any law of God o'erleaps,
He is of God;" these proud men cry;
"This Jesus doth His laws defy!"
But others, men of candid mind
Though strait by prejudice confined,
Said, "How may a man such marvel do
Except he doth God's ways pursue?"
Disputings follow; they divide,

Some this and some the other side
Espousing in their heat;—"Let be,
What says yon blind man made to see?"
But long has he made up his mind,
Nor hesitates fit word to find:
"He is a prophet;" cried he, sure:
The Jews would not this word endure,
And reviled the man: then, "'Tis not true
That the man was born blind; go, you,
Find out his parents; they will tell."
In panic came they, knowing well
The fate of them who opposed the Jews,—
Cast out of synagogue, who refuse
Agreement with the rulers. Fear
Gives counsel ere the two appear:
"He is our son and was born blind;
How sees he now, is to our mind
A mystery; but let him tell,
He is of age to answer well."
So said the fearful parents, knowing
That to own Christ were their undoing.

LV

The seeing man and the Pharisees

A SECOND time they called the man, made free
Of the joys of light and vision. Suave their speech,
As of men with an end to gain:
A Pharisee. Give praise
To God, my friend, who in mercy wrought for thee;
We understand thy will to bless this man,
But thou know'st him not as we do; we're informed
Most surely that he's a sinner.
Elihu. Be it so;
Sinner or not, I know not: this I know,—
Whereas I was blind, I see.
Pharisee. A curious thing!
Physicians may be able to testify
To sudden sight attained by the long blind;
Or, hap, He used some unguent magical:
What did He do to thee? How ope'd thine eyes?
Elihu. Why ask again? I told you even now;
Could words be plainer? What hindered you to hear?

Would ye hear the tale again, the wondrous tale
Of how a man sat darkened all his days,
And One came by, and—sudden, he saw the sun!
Hap, ye would learn 't by heart, convinced at last
And meet to be His disciples!

Pharisee. How dar'st thou, man,
Swine of the common people, lift thy voice
Against thy people's rulers! How dar'st mock
At the learned as were they fools like such as thou!
Pah! fellow, how canst understand, confute
With muddy wits the doctors of the Law?
Out, out upon thee! His disciple thou,
And hast no place in the temple. Go thou forth,
Herd with the excommunicate! For us,
Hear, thou blasphemer! Moses' disciples, we;
We know that God hath spoken to Moses—else,
Wherefore the temple, all our solemn rites,
The Law itself,—all sacrifice? This man,
This outcast of the people, who is He?
Trust us, we've looked the matter up: No place
Owns the impostor, never father hath;
And this, the nameless, homeless runagate,
Thou wouldst have the rulers honour!

Elihu. Why, indeed,
Here is a marvellous thing; ye know Him not,

Ye who hold the counsels of God, and deal to us
With niggard hand and slow! And yet this Man,
Alien, contemn'd of you, hath ope'd mine eyes!
Not learned am I, but this thing I do know,—
All power belongs to God, as ye allow;
'Tis God alone can ope a blind man's eyes;
So far, are we agreed: but this I know,—
Thing ye forget, or never understood!—
The righteous man who does the will of God,
He hath the ear of the HIGHEST: when he prays,
His prayer is granted to the uttermost;
But there be those besiege Heaven's gates in vain;
No password, missile, 's theirs to gain access;
God doth not sinners hear. Take th' case in point,—
Not since the world began has it been heard
That any ope'd the eyes of one born blind:
A new thing this—a marvel in the world!
Were this Man not from God, nought could He do;
His clay, His washings, were an idle play:
How say ye, then, a sinner hath done this?
Hark ye, for once, to a plain man's reasonings.

Pharisees. (Gnashing their teeth in rage, running at him,
With claws outstretched as they would tear out eyes:)
Thou, thou, unclean, defiled and born in sin,
Ignorant, base—a beggar at our gates,

Dost thou indeed teach us?
                                        And they cast him out:
Poor wretch, he went his way, in worse case, sure,
Than when, a blind man, he sat there and
    begged:
Full well he knew the measure of his woe;
No cheerful greeting henceforth was for him
From friend or passing stranger. None might
    aid;
Not father or mother might now give him bread;
None might employ, or proffer him an alms:
What misery his could equal? Wherefore was't
That with this doom upon him he went glad,
Soft in the memory of one sweet thing,—
A touch upon his eyes, a word that bade,—
Thing so sufficing that, his woes forgot,
Purpose and joy shone in his seeing eyes;—
He would find Jesus.

LVI

The vision

He went with singing heart and fond desire
To see the face had blessed him in the dark;
To find a vent for all that glowing fire
Of love at his heart. He watched; he listened; hark,
Was that *His* voice? By sight he could not mark
The Man in the crowd who, speaking, bade him see:
But as he went he sang like any lark,
So good it was a seeing man to be;
So good to walk the world in great expectancy.

But when true love awakes in any heart,
Another heart, attending, feels the glow:
None seeking Christ can have a lonely part;
To seek who seeks Him, quick the Lord doth go,—
The Lord of love; full surely doth He know
When one desires Him as the water-brook,
The hunted stag solicits. As waters flow
Together, meeting in a shady nook,
The erst-blind man and Christ joined in a single look,—

The two made one! Christ met him on his
quest
Whom He had gone to seek; and asked him
straight
That question which to answer is the hest
Laid on each son of man; nor bid him wait
For help should come to ease his poor estate,—
But,—"Dost thou on the Son of God believe?"
Awed by demand momentous, intimate,
But hungering due knowledge to receive,—
"Who is he, Lord?" he answered instant, to
relieve

The intolerable ecstasy in him:
"Thou seest Him," said Christ, "and He it is
That speaks with thee:" whereat his eyes grew
dim
With sudden swelling tears of holy bliss;—
"Lord, I believe!" he cried, who had thought
to miss
The common sights of life, or bird, or tree,
When, lo, his eyes were opened, and to this—
The Vision of his Saviour! Thus thought he
Communing with his thankful heart all secretly.

LVII

Evidence

(*The disciple*)

"THAT, whereas I was blind, now I do see,"—
The erst-blind man made answer when men sought
To investigate that work which had been wrought
On him, unhappy. Behold, for you and me,
The sole reply for who, the mystery
Of that change wrought in us, would understand:
Our "evidence"—imperious, they demand:
And we, long blind, can only say,—"We see!"

But, ah, the difference! we had been blind,
Soliciting the world for things of nought;
Receiving from the grudging hand unkind
Mean scraps of pleasure, meat, for which we sought,
Poor suppliants. Now, what is this we find?—
All things are ours through Him who for us wrought!

BOOK V

CHRIST, OUR LIFE

LVIII

The silly sheep

Ye think the sheep are witless, cannot know;
Respond to any call, and ready go
After whoso will lead them;

Poor silly sheep, that scarce are safe in fold
Enclosed by shepherd who hath duly told
Their number, one by one there;

Without are robbers, who shall climb the fence,
Get in to the poor sheep on fond pretence
That they have come to feed them;

There is that cometh not in by the door
But climbeth up some other way, the more
Privily to destroy them;

But, duly by the door, the Shepherd, see,
Comes for his sheep; the porter opens free;
The sheep, they gather round him:

Their shepherd's voice is music in their ear;
He calls each one by name; they have no fear,
But come in haste to follow.

He leads them forth where pleasant places be;
His sheep who know His voice will never flee
Their shepherd who doth love them.

A stranger, trespassing, invades the fold,
And calls the sheep out masterful and bold,
But see, they will not have him.

They flee and in remotest places hide;
Nor may this stranger in their midst abide,—
They know not th' voice of strangers.

Frederick Shields

THE GOOD SHEPHERD

By permission of The Autotype Fine Art Co. Ltd.,
74 New Oxford Street, London, W.C.

LIX

The sheep and the fold

Who be the sheep, say ye, and what the fold,
And what the door by which they enter in?
Where be those thieves and robbers overbold
Would break in by offence and ruthless sin?
Give ear and ye shall understand the tale,
And how the Shepherd shall at last prevail.

The sheep, they are My people; all who hear
My voice and follow,—not Israel alone;
I gather these, and close them in from fear
By the fence which is My Church; and every stone
In the fence is tried and fitted; at the gate,
Is faithful porter set to watch and wait.

Long, long ago, I folded these My sheep;
But heedless watchers hungry wolves let in,
Ravening to slay the flock which none did keep;
Now am I come their rescue to begin:
The door am I through which My sheep shall go;
Their shepherd, too, who leads them to and fro.

I know My sheep; though they be silly, weak,
Yet not to other voices lend they ear
Of thieves and robbers rude; though they be meek,
These hear they not nor suffer to draw near;
But when their Shepherd calls, with answering bleat—
They haste them to lie down about His feet.

I am the door; who enters in by Me
Is welcomed, cherished, guarded from all ill;
Would he go forth to taste the pastures free
Of knowledge, poems, pictures, at his will?
He goes and comes unhindered; everywhere,
He finds green pastures in his Shepherd's care.

But they who be not shepherds do not so;
They steal the pasture, kill the helpless sheep;
Like Jeshurun, they fat and thriving grow,
They kick and hurt the flock they're set to keep:
And from strange pastures bring they poisonous weeds
Of doctrine, precept,—grown in other meads.

But I am the Good Shepherd; in Mine arm
The little tender lambs I shield from cold;
The feeble silly sheep keep safe from harm;
Retrieve those wanderers who have waxed too bold;
Ask ye what sustenance I to them supply?
Life, and more life, and life abundantly.

LX

The sheep and the Shepherd

AND these, My cherished sheep,—how happy, they,
Fulfilled with life, come forth and follow Me:
Sweet music, joy of living, on that day
They hear My voice, shall for these simple be:
The world is theirs, nor anything denied
To the flock that followed when their Shepherd cried.

The sheep are safe; the Shepherd, what of Him?
The sheep go full; the Shepherd, hath He need?
Poor sheep, scarce may their understanding dim
Perceive the cost; they take with little heed
The gift of His life their Shepherd, offering, holds,
That He may keep His sheep from alien folds.

See you, not thus the hireling behaves;
The sheep are not his own; when danger nears,

Beholding the wolf coming, loud he raves
  And flees distract by his own coward fears;
The wolves—disaster, danger—snatch the sheep;
The hireling's only care, himself to keep.

The hireling, what hath he of that love
  Between those two who one another know?
I know Mine own; Mine own know Me; above
  The world's loud cries they hear when I speak low,
And haste to Me, their Shepherd; for their sake
I give the life those robbers think to take:

E'en as the Father knows Me, know I these,
  And as I know the Father, know they Me:
Therefore roam they at large and dwell at ease;
  The Truth, their generous pasture, makes them free;
And yet, love-tethered, keep they by the door
Where they go in and out for evermore.

These sheep are safely herded in the fold;
  But there be others scattered far and wide
Waiting the Shepherd in the dark and cold:
  These must I go and bring, nor be denied:
And they shall hear My voice, by Me be led,
And in one fold securely shepherded.

Nor think that I alone for them have care;
  The Father loves the silly scattered sheep;
And He loves Me for this, that I would share
  Fulness of life with these He bids Me keep:
For these, I lay down life; for these I take
My life again; and no man shall Me make:

This is the Father's will, that I should die
  For the dear flock which unto Me He gave;
And His commandment cheerfully will I
  Perform to the uttermost these sheep to save:
Nor think that ye to kill Me have the power;
I *give* My life when HE appoints the hour.

LXI

The Jews talk

THESE words of sheep and shepherd heard the Jews;
Their restless hearts within them witness bore,
As sheep that have no shepherd, doubt-distressed;
But who takes counsel with his secret heart
When he hath a part to play in men's affairs?
Their part, to save the temple, condemn the Man
Who made things seem quite other than they knew—
Belittled all their rights, relaxed their claims.
Jew. Why hear ye him, good people? He is mad;
Nay, hath a devil who prompts Him with large words
Of sheep and shepherd when ye look for sense;
What means the Man, I pray you? Rulers, priests,
These be the people's shepherds; pasture fit
In sacrificial rites is spread for you,
In teachings of the law by your scribes set forth;
Aye, thieves and robbers they, who would break through fold

Which encloses Israel : heaven's curse on them,
On this Man, every man who would lead astray
The chosen of the Lord!

Another. A devil, see you,
Must needs speak of his own; must lie and hate.
Whence hath a devil words of love and life
And healing for the nations? Take ye heed;
An awful thing it were to fight against God!
What if HE sent a sign? Can devils ope
The eyes of a man born blind? I pray you, pause.

LXII

The vagrant sheep

(*The disciple*)

SURE, I, a sheep of the Good Shepherd's fold;
One day I 'scape Him for the uplands cold
Which entice my silly fancy with the hope
Of pasture new and delicate, free scope:
Eager I leave the fold nor meet the eye
Of Him in charge as stealthy I creep by:
Lo, those high places difficult of ascent
Yield nought for famished creature's nourishment:
I bleat in desolate terror; soon, He comes;
The Shepherd follows there, where His sheep roams.

Another day I spy a pasture green,—
Rich, luscious eating for a sheep I ween;
I steal away whilst He doth play His lute,
And the good sheep lie round entranced and mute:
Soon taste I of that herbage coarse and rude;
And fain would leave it, with disgust imbued:

But I am sinking, may not step or rise,
A rank swamp holding me my strength defies:—
The shepherd comes and rescues me again,
And tender bears me to the peaceful plain.

Sure, never would I wander more, you cry?
Ah, sheep, they be but silly! A wood hard by
Hedged a fair lawn, and I must needs essay
To reach that pasture green, though hard the way;
I had not penetrated far the grove,
When, lo, I was locked fast; I could not move
For thorns that held me, tore me, made me bleed;
I cried and vexed me sore that with slight heed
I had involved me in so hazardous place:
The Shepherd came and freed me of dear grace.

The barren heights of intellect erst wooed,—
Thither the tender Shepherd me pursued:
Lusts of the flesh, indulgence, swamped my soul,—
My Saviour brought me under sweet control:
The cares of life, as cruel thorns, held back,—
Brought safe to Christ His meads I knew no lack:
And now, a sheep secure in pastures green,
My soul expands in the so beauteous scene
Displayed where'er the Shepherd leads His flock—
Now, to full pastures, now, to sheltering Rock.

LXIII

Between the festivals

JERUSALEM draws the Lord as the eye of snake
Compels the fluttering bird to seek her doom:
Where wandered He between those festivals,
Autumn's and Winter's high solemnities?
We have no word. On Jordan's further side,
Or in and out the dales of Galilee,
Might men a group of mournful aspect pass,
Wending 'neath the shadow of a cloud all saw—
Though One alone had prescience?

Did Christ repeat to the Twelve that lore of life
He had unfolded at the earlier Feast?
Once more, did He proclaim that men must judge,—
Each for himself discern the thing that's true?
Again, the Water of Life did He offer free,
Or, manifest to them the Light of the World?
The days draw in and He must soon depart;
But not before He had left the Truth with the Twelve—
A sacred legacy, lodged in place secure,
The hearts of those whose errand was to proclaim

Those mysteries all must know an be they saved:
How urgent was't that these should understand,
These Twelve who should go forth to th' ends
of the world
To cry aloud His doctrine—shew His life!

LXIV

The months of teaching

Time sped; the days, weeks, hours, escaped alike
From them would hold and them would haste
their flight;
To Christ and His Twelve, how ominous each fall
Of night on the round world! For the Twelve,
poor souls,
An awful presage darkened all their days;
More awful, that they might not read the signs
Which the Master, day by day, displayed to them,
Had patience with them for they were so slow,
And Himself went lacking their fond sympathy,—
He, sore bestead by the awful certainties
That hour by hour pressed heavier: day by day,
Was time retrenched for th' fulfilment of that
task
Laid on Him ere He died: How teach these
men
The mysteries it was their part to know,
The while they brought no stomach to the task,—
Too wrapped in gloom of coming grief to think,
Or set their minds to comprehend the words
Which the Master spake in solitary wastes

Whither He led them those dull winter months?
And as they go, He notes the silly sheep,
Each flock about its shepherd safe from wolves;
And knows, that not to the wolves would He
    leave His own;
Should not He lead them still and still provide?

LXV

In Solomon's Porch

Then, were they idle, all those words the Lord
Had dropped amongst the Pharisees, the Scribes?
The words of truth, eternal, cannot pass;
Remain they with the hearer evermore,
To save him or to damn.
The Lord withdrawn,
The words He spake remained, and raised a din
Of controversy whence no issue was;
For men believed and knew, or else refused
And belied the sacred truth, self-evidenced.
For the Feast of Dedication, Christ came up:
They saw Him walking there in Solomon's Porch
With the Twelve, His chosen friends; would speak Him fair;
As the Lord walks, a curious group surrounds,—
Nay, separates between Him and His own,—
Men pawing the air with eloquent hands, and close,
Into the face serene of the Son of Man,
Thrusting disordered visages, agog,
Not as they'd fain believe, for very truth,
But for victory over this interloper,—
Nought yesterday, to-day, in all men's mouths!

LXVI

The controversy renewed : eternal life

The Jews. How long hold'st us in suspense?
If Thou be Christ,
Tell us so plainly that we may believe;
(*So, Herod, when he sought the young Child's life*)—
Thou hidest under cover of vain words,
Figures and allegories of no intent,
Or deepest import as men shall receive:
A Shepherd? What's a shepherd, save a hind
Engaged to lead sheep forth, and keep and fetch?
Thou playest with grave doctors of the law
With Thy vain talk of shepherd, light and door!
Speak plainly if Thou'dst have us hold Thee sane!
THE LORD. I told you, and ye believe not: all the works
I have done before you in My Father's name,—
In His name, for, indeed, they be His works
That He practiseth continually the while
He blesseth, feedeth, restoreth life to men,—
These works I do are tongues to tell of Me;
Hath ever man rejoicing ta'en his way
As the sun in heaven, shedding life and light?
What ails you that ye will not understand?

If more than man's My words, if more My works,
Why, what remains to think?
The Jews. Thou reasonest well;
The silly multitude must needs believe
And follow as Thou lead'st; but we're no sheep,—
Unreasoning souls to follow where we're led!
THE LORD. There spake ye true; ye are no sheep of Mine;
See you, My sheep discern 'mongst many voices
The voice of Him, their Shepherd; I know them;
For them, they watch their Shepherd's eye; read they,
Therein, authority and tenderness,—
Rule, each must follow; love, which embraces each;
They follow Me; and, lo, as they come, meek,
I give them of My own—eternal life!
The Jews. "Eternal life!" what's that? The pot of gold
The children look for where the rainbow ends!
Gav'st Thou them bread to stay their stomachs on,
Poor wretches, 'twere a seemlier gift for them!
But, see'st Thou, those sorry sheep of Thine,
They go, as Thou, in peril of their lives:
Who scorn the Law shall perish by the Law;
What then of th' eternal life Thou giv'st?
THE LORD. Kill ye,
Yet live they still; ye follow, track and seize,
Yet never from My hand shall one of these

Be snatched by you—or all the powers of hell.
The Jews. They die and do not perish—what is this?
A madman's ravings or a charlatan's guile
Uttered to deceive the people?
THE LORD. Blind are ye,
And will not see the truth! Talk to the blind
Of splendour of sunset-skies, thou dost but rave;
Poor man who knows not colour, what to him
Your greens and purples, crimsons, violet tints?
All is but silly talk! And you, My friends,
Who take no count of God in all your thought,
You think on life as blind men think on light—
'Tis nought to you! Believe Me, life is God,
And where is God, there is eternal life.
The Jews. Mark how He shirks the point;—we spake of these,
The ignorant multitude; and He lessons us
With that which children learn at mothers' knees—
That life is of God!
THE LORD. Aye, life is of God; and HE
Hath given life to these poor sheep of Mine,
My Father's gift to Me; wherefore, I say,
That none shall snatch them from Me; there is One
Who keeps them, cherishes, spoon-feeds with life:
My Father is greater than all; what do ye then?

The Jews. That God is great, all know; but who art Thou?

THE LORD. I and the Father are one.

The Jews. We told you so!
Hear His rank blasphemy! Shall this man live,
To mock Jehovah and the people's rulers?

LXVII

They take up stones to stone Him

Again, demoniac-wrath o'ermastered them,
As on that other day when Christ proclaimed,—
"From everlasting to everlasting, I am God;"
As on that day, tore they cobbles from the street
Wherewith to stone their God, made manifest:
What withheld their impious hands? a prudent fear
Of Rome, who brooked not trespass on her laws?
To th' winds with prudence! cries your man in wrath:
Was it the eye of Christ, deterrent, held,
As dog in leash, these savage, venomous?
That we might see our Lord as stood He there,
This Man, our Peace, in the tempest of men's hate!
Calm reasoned words, as oil, He drops on them,
And they, willing or wroth, must needs hear Him.

How strange the transposition, could the man
In the prisoner's dock sudden transfer himself
To the awful Bench of the Judge, he, go below
To the place of the accused! So fared these men

Self-constituted judges: their upraised hand
Ready to launch the murderous stone, was held:
Constrained, they heard the accusing words of
Him,
The Judge, austere and calm.

THE LORD. Many good works
From the Father—His own acts—have I performed,
To convince, compel you to perceive the truth:
Are works of mercy the offences ye condemn?
What then of God, whose mercies every morn
Are poured unstinted in the laps of men?
Is this your return to Me who do His works?
And for which of these would ye stone Me?

The Jews. For a good work
We stone Thee not, but for blasphemy,—the last
Worst sin a man can do,—we Thee arraign;
Wilt have it, this our charge;—that Thou, being
man,
Makest Thyself as God.

THE LORD. O fools and blind,
Who know not their estate, how great it is,
But hold them bounded by the flesh, its needs
And fond desires, how indeed can they perceive
The open secret of the Father's face,
The errand of the Son! Have ye not read
In your law, (and the Scriptures cannot be
broken),
"I said, Ye are gods"? What sense, then, bear
the words,—

Have ye ta'en thought to know? If they be gods
To whom came the word of God, you, an ye will,
If they who hear be children of the Highest,
What then of Him whom the Father sanctified
E'en for this thing, to discover their estate
To men; to say to them—"Ye are gods; abide
Then in your Father's house and work His will."
The Jews. No gods are we, and thou, thou hast a devil
Who heapeth blasphemy on blasphemy!
Thou hast no part or lot in the Nation!
THE LORD. Why?
Because I said, I am the Son of God?
Bethink you; use your reasoning mind and judge:
A man's works testify,—show what he is;
If I do not the works of God, ye are right,
I am not the Son of God; but if I do,
Then, let the works themselves convince, not I;
Believe the works, so shall ye understand
That the Father is in Me, and in Him, I
Do move and have My being.

But who were they
To comprehend supernal mysteries,—
How the unseen God should dwell in visible Form,
And how the visible Christ had His dwelling-place,
Serene, unchanging, in the unseen God:

And how of all men it is said, "Ye are gods,"
Even so far as ye will have it so—
Receive the filial portion: how, in Christ,
In absolute measure was the Word fulfilled,
For He, of God, as God could comprehend:—
Those narrow souls, what was all this to them,
Each tied and bound fast in a web of schemes
For his own aggrandisement?

Again, they seek
To lay hold on the Lord, and He went from them.

Photo, Alinari *Taddeo Gaddi and Simone Memmi*

I. ALLEGORIA FILOSOFICA DELLA RELIGIONE CATTOLICA

Photo, Alinari *Taddeo Gaddi and Simone Memmi*

II. ALLEGORIA FILOSOFICA DELLA RELIGIONE CATTOLICA

LXVIII

I said, Ye are gods

O WONDROUS magnanimity, divine,
Of Thy sayings, Son of Man! Thou tak'st a word
Which those vindictive Jews have often heard,—
And, straight, an added star in heaven doth shine!

Godlike retort to all that captious twine
Of learning, logic, rivalry, that raged
As fire of hate in their breast, not once assuaged,
By the cool breath of truth's discernment fine!—

"I am not God, ye say? Nay, gods are ye,
Children of the Most High in your vast power
Of Thought—to range all time in one short hour,
Of Love—to cherish the least things that be:

I come that ye may realise your dower
Of potent godhood—manifest in Me!"

LXIX

At the pool

A SPOT there was dear to the heart of Christ,
A place where many had kept holy tryst,—
That pool where John baptized, where troubled
men
Had sought that washing which makes clean
again.
There, beyond Jordan, did the Lord abide,
From the vexing of the Jews, constrained to hide:
Here, many came to Him;—from city street,
From all the country side, the people meet
To hear the words of Jesus, see each sign
Which to the open soul proved Him divine.
For many of these, dear, earlier memories clung
To the spot where on the words of John they'd
hung:
The people spake together: No sign did John,
But this Man hath fulfilled them, every one,—
The words John spake of Him.
And, day by day,
The people heard and spake and went their way,
And came again to hear the words of life;

So, many believed on Him, for all that strife
Of words in the city raised by Pharisees.

If John be present, how joyful now he sees,
With the larger eyes of the spirit-life, this grace
His King hath done him, sweet as an embrace!
That Christ should gather with His royal hand
Fruit from that seed he scattered in the land.

LXX

The Raising of Lazarus

a

The house of a friend

THE house of a friend! How good to know,
In hours of anxious drear distress,
That there's a place where we may go
For company in loneliness;
Where sympathetic hand shall press
Our own when life is hard to bear;—
A sheltered still and sweet recess
Where we may come for smile or tear,
Of welcome well-assured ere yet our steps draw near!

Sweet home of Bethany, our thought
Lovely and pleasant finds thy ways!
We bless thee for the solace brought
By thee to Christ in heavy days:
Thou green spot in the desert, praise
We the gracious family there:
Fit subject for the poets' lays,
A modest household free from care,—
Place where the Master found refreshment sweet and rare.

LXXI

The message sent

β

Happy the home that hath a friend
Who makes its pains and joys his own;
Who hastes on wings of love to lend
Help, service, sympathy; alone,
No household suffers nor makes moan
For any sorrow or dismay
Where a friend's countenance is known:
O'ertaken by a grievous day,
Straight send they for their friend, assured what part he'll play.

Not set apart from sorrow, e'en
That home beloved of Christ: for there,
Two loving sisters watched, I ween,
A fevered bed,—where heavy Care
Took turns in watching with Despair:
Yet not without hope the sisters grieve;
"Go, fetch our Friend; for He will share
This anguish with us; will relieve,
Nay, cure our brother, for—He loves and we believe!"

LXXII

The message received

γ

Ah me, the mother's woe, whose son
Is sentenced to the surgeon's knife;
While his petitions ceaseless run,
"O mother, mother, spare my life!"
And keeps he up the useless strife,
And deems his mother hard and cold,
That not for all his urgings, rife
With blame and love, dare she make bold
To bid the surgeon cease,—who is her hope's stronghold!

The footsore runners found the Lord;
The burning message spake they true:
"He whom Thou lov'st is sick," their word;
And all were sure what He would do:
The disciples near their Master drew
Expecting word, "Let us make speed,
Go we to cheer the sisters two!"
But Christ, as one who took no heed,
For two whole days delayed; the while His heart did bleed!

LXXIII

The Master delays

δ

But the Twelve, chief in the Church, were there,
Who needs must learn God's secret ways;
To them spake Christ,—"Have ye no fear;
This sickness shall be for God's praise:
Nor blame ye what seem vain delays,—
Needful, the Christ to manifest:"
See, the Lord's countenance betrays
The love He bears that household blest,—
How He refrains Himself that He might serve them best!

"Come, go we to Judæa again:"
"Rabbi, they sought to stone Thee there!"
"A man from his work shall not refrain
While daylight lasts; he is aware,
Nor stumbleth in the light;—Prepare,
For Lazarus, our friend, now sleeps
And I go to awaken him." They stare;
"Nay, sleep is good," say they, "none weeps
For such reprieve:" "he is dead:" saith He who all souls keeps.

LXXIV

"Let us go"

THE father who his son would train
May not choose pleasant paths to tread;
Behoves him sometimes teach through pain;
Through trial, up, the boy is led.
"For your sakes, I am glad his bed
Was not watched over by his Friend,
That ye may believe that word I said,—
'I am the Life': come, see the end."
Said Didymus, "To die with Him we too will
wend."

Two dismal watchers shared that home,
Sat with the sisters in their woe;
Should doubt and sorrow ever roam
From place whose lord had been laid low?
Four days had he been gone, as though
Labourers had carried from the field:
Death came, and did his errand; lo,
No comfort might kind neighbours yield:
That only Friend with help, He kept himself
concealed.

LXXV

"If Thou hadst been here"

ζ

Who knoweth not the weariness
Of friendly futile words in grief?
The sisters heard in listlessness
Those Jews' stale speech nor found relief:
A whisper rose that He, their Chief,
At last was on His tardy way:
Martha went out to Him; and brief
And bitter speech urged eager way:—
"Master, by loitering late, didst Thou my brother slay!"

But, ere the hasty words were out
Her eyes beheld the Face divine;
Perceived she with uneasy doubt
He yet might do some work benign,—
For sure He had the Father's ear:
Too late for her! she must resign
The brother so exceeding dear:—
"Lazarus shall rise again: then weep not thou, nor fear."

LXXVI

" I am the Resurrection "

η

How cold the comfort brought by hope
Of future good for present ill!
The mourner too could treasures ope
Of faith, religion,—vain to fill
Her empty heart: " I wait until
The last great resurrection shout
To see him if it be God's will."
We, faithless Mourner, bless that doubt
Which evoked the word, we may—nor live nor die without!

" I am the Resurrection, I, the Life:"—
Ah, blessèd woman, that thine ear,
Prepared by sorrow's poignant strife,
Should first those words momentous hear!
Thou learn'dst,—the resurrection's near;
Thou learn'dst,—the rising from the dead
Is all one act with living here
For who receives that word Christ said,—
" He who believes in Me, alive, through death is led."

LXXVII

"Believest thou this?"

θ

"Believest thou this?" "Yea, Lord," said she,
Arrived through portals of the grave
At the very gate of Life where He
Stood holding out the life He gave
To all who knew that life to crave:
"Yea, Lord," she said, scarce yet aware
Of Christ's omnipotence to save,—
"Thou art the Christ, I know; and share
In the hope Thou bring'st from God to heal the world's despair."

Straight runs she home, assured and eased
Of the soreness of her rebel mind;
And whispers Mary, inly pleased
With the message to her lips assigned,—
"The Master has come; well He divined
How life hath gone from us; saith He,—
'I am the Life, He that doth bind
The dead and living; both shall be
Alive for evermore, believe they but in Me.'"

LXXVIII

"Jesus wept"

i

"The Master is here and calls for thee:"
With solace came the words; she rose
And hastened forth her Lord to see:
The friendly Jews cried, "See, she goes
There by the grave to weep her woes;
Let's go that we may also mourn:"
She sees the Lord, and sorrow flows
From eyes grown used to grief's return:
"Hadst Thou been here, my Lord, the grave
were not his bourne!"

Nay, why doth the Redeemer "groan"?
Is sorrow grievous to Him, too,
To whom the Dead are as seed sown
That ampler life they may renew?
He stands there troubled Who can do
Beyond the bravest hopes of men:
They weep as their fond thoughts pursue
The friend they shall not see again:
And *Jesus wept*,—o'erwhelmed by all men's
sorrows then!

LXXIX

"Said I not"

K

"See how He loved him!" cried the Jews;
A common sorrow touched their heart:
"Would He that hath such power refuse
To hinder that our friend depart
Had He been here in time? What art
Can save our Lazarus, four days dead?
No more, alas, we'll meet in mart!"
Thus talked they while the Lord they led
To the tomb where Lazarus lay; and there, strange word He said:—

"Take ye away the stone:" she cries,
Provident Martha,—"he offends
By this time, Lord, for see, he lies
Decaying these four days:" she ends
Words which bewray how far transcends
Her earlier speech the thing she feels!
'Tis thus emotion colour lends
To words but not our heart reveals:
"Said I not unto thee"—saith He, who tender deals.

LXXX

"Thy judgements are like the great deep"

λ

As fluttering birds just 'scaped the nest,
Half blinded, baffled, by wide air,
Make tiny flight, then sink to rest
Fall'n in some ditch which chances there;—
E'en so our timid fancies fare
In that vast ocean of deep thought
Thou launchest us upon;—scarce dare
We seize a hope we ne'er had sought,
Or hold secure the bliss that Word to men hath brought!

"I am the light,"—we think we see;
"I am the door,"—we peer within;
"I am the life,"—Lord, ever be
Our life to save from death of sin!
"I am the resurrection,"—win
We, for all our thinking, scarce
A hint of all enclosed within
The casket of that word; nay, worse,
Vain words of would-be faith, like Martha, we rehearse.

LXXXI

"Lift us up for ever"

μ

POSTPONE we till some far-off day—
That last great day when men shall rise—
Marvel, the Master would display
Constant before our wondering eyes:—
The life we hold in Him defies
Death's last assault; we go to bed;
In dust awhile our body lies;
Our friends bewail us;—whilst we're led
By our Risen Lord to seats whence Death flies,
vanquishéd.

And every day, behold, we fall;
But, lo, that germ of life we hold
May not be weighted by the pall
Of custom, or of death as cold;
We rise, in our Redeemer bold;
Where there is life needs must it rise;
No cerement shall the soul enfold;
The strong truth lifts us to the skies:
Lo, resurrection is—our life in amplest guise.

LXXXII

"Lazarus, come forth"

v

THEY moved the stone:—He lifted eyes,
And gave the Father words of praise
That they about should realise
How God was with Him in His ways,—
Both in His hastenings and delays:
Then with authority He cried,
"Lazarus, come forth": and through four days
Of distance heard he who had died:
Obedient came he forth in graveclothes bound and tied.

Whence came he? From some joy remote
Where his shy spirit scarce at ease
Looked on, as timid child will note
His elders' games, wishing to please,
And getting easier by degrees:
Was 't thus with Lazarus out there?
As happy boys and girls, were these
Whose bliss he had come far to share?
And did he fond regards to his dear "living" spare?

Photo, Braun *Bonifazio*

THE RAISING OF LAZARUS

LXXXIII

The man who knew

o

THERE is no word of all he learned
Come down, us, living souls, to cheer:
Nor know we how his fond heart burned
Within him to see Jesus near:
The silence of the grave, the fear,
Remains about him :—but a word,
Late said by One who held him dear,
Offers the key by Christ conferred
On such as, understanding, heard ;—
"I said, ye are gods,"—that word late spoken by
the Lord.

The schoolboy learns with grievous pains;
Full hard the lessons for him set;
Not yet may he count up his gains,
Enough for him his task to get:
Here was a man whose heart had met
With loving comprehension all
The teaching of the Lord: regret
Found no place in him when the call
"Friend, go up higher," came: he turned him
to the wall :—
What uttermost fulfilment did the man befal?
Full knowing, loving, living, and the Lord God
in all?

LXXXIV

" Ye shall be as gods"

" I said, Ye are gods"

" Poor your estate ! ye do as ye are bid,
Nor dare ask the Creator why 'tis so ;
He chooseth not that His reasons ye shall know,
And, questioned ye, full surely were ye chid ;
Knowledge and power from you, blind souls, are hid ;
Would ye be as gods, acquaint with all below ?
Come eat this fruit ; so shall your knowledge grow ;
Sure, of ill-will, the apple is forbid ! "

The ready ear is charmed with wily tale :—
Men fain assert themselves as gods to be :
They swell in pride and break in misery !
" Ye are gods," saith Christ, " and certain, ye shall know ;
Your power to love and serve shall never fail ;
God knows ; God serves ; and ye as gods shall go."

NOTE

THE PICTURE, LA FILOSOFICA DELLA RELIGIONE CATTOLICA

Mr. Ruskin has done a great service to modern thought in interpreting for us the harmonious and ennobling scheme of education and philosophy recorded upon one quarter of what he calls the "Vaulted Book,"[1] *i.e.*, the Spanish Chapel attached to the Church of Sta. Maria Novella, in Florence.

"The descent of the Holy Ghost is on the left hand (of the roof) as you enter. The Madonna and Disciples are gathered in an upper chamber: underneath are the Parthians, Medes, Elamites, &c., who hear them speak in their own tongues. Three dogs are in the foreground—their mythic purpose, to mark the share of the lower animals in the gentleness given by the outpouring of the Spirit of Christ. . . . On this and the opposite side of the Chapel are

[1] *Mornings in Florence* (Allen).

represented by Simon Memmi's hand, the teaching power of the Spirit of God and the saving power of the Christ of God in the world, according to the understanding of Florence in his time.

"We will take the side of intellect first. Beneath the pouring forth of the Holy Spirit in the point of the arch beneath are the three Evangelical Virtues. Without these, says Florence, you can have no science. Without Love, Faith, and Hope—no intelligence. Under these are the four Cardinal Virtues . . . Temperance, Prudence, Justice, Fortitude. Under these are the great Prophets and Apostles. . . . Under the line of Prophets, as powers summoned by their voices, are the mythic figures of the seven theological or spiritual and the seven geological or natural sciences; and under the feet of each of them the figure of its Captain-teacher to the world."

Our immediate concern is with the seven mythic figures representing the natural sciences, and with the figure of the Captain-teacher of each. First we have Grammar, a gracious figure teaching three Florentine children; and, beneath, Priscian. Next, Rhetoric, strong, calm and cool; and, below, the figure of Cicero with a quiet beautiful face. Next, Logic, with perfect pose of figure and lovely face; and beneath her, Aristotle—intense keenness of search in his half-closed eyes. Next, Music, with head inclined in intent listening to the sweet and solemn strains she is producing from her antique instrument; and underneath, Tubal Cain, not Jubal, as the inventor of harmony—perhaps the most marvellous record that Art has produced of the impact of a great idea upon the soul of a man but semi-civilised. Astronomy succeeds, with majestic brow and upraised hand, and below her, Zoroaster, exceedingly beautiful—"the delicate Persian head made softer still by the elaborately wreathed silken hair." Next, Geometry, looking down, considering some practical problem, with her carpenter's square in her hand, and below her, Euclid. And lastly, Arithmetic, holding two fingers up in the act of calculating, and under her, Pythagoras wrapped in the science of number.

The Florentines of the Middle Ages believed, not only that the seven Liberal Arts were fully under the direct outpouring of the Holy Ghost, but that every fruitful idea, every original conception, whether in Euclid, or grammar, or music, was a direct inspiration from the Holy Spirit, with no consideration as to whether the person so inspired named himself by the name of God, or recognised whence his inspiration came. It seems to me that there exists no better comment upon the saying, "I said, ye are gods," than this expression of mediæval philosophy as embraced by the Church.

C. M. M.

INDEX

Of Subjects and References to Passages in the Holy Scriptures on which each of the Poems is founded.

BOOK I

OF FORGIVENESS

I

II

III

BOOK III

THE WATER OF LIFE

LXX

The Raising of Lazarus

v

Printed by BALLANTYNE, HANSON & Co.
Edinburgh & London